BLOSSOMS FOLD

TOWNWELL FOLD

FARMERS FOLD

MITRE FOLD

FOLD STREET

WOOLPACK STREET

THE FOLDS OF
WOLVERHAMPTON

BLOSSOMS FOLD
TOWNWELL FOLD
FARMERS FOLD
MITRE FOLD
FOLD STREET
WOOLPACK STREET

THE FOLDS OF
WOLVERHAMPTON

ANTHONY PERRY

BREWIN BOOKS

First published by
Brewin Books Ltd, 56 Alcester Road,
Studley, Warwickshire B80 7LG in 2005
www.brewinbooks.com
Reprinted September 2005

ISBN 1 85858 265 2

A Cataloguing in Publication Record
for this title is available from the British Library.

Typeset in Baskerville
Printed in Great Britain by
SupaPrint (Redditch) Limited

CONTENTS

FOREWORD
Professor Carl Chinn MBE

Streets fascinate me. Usually they are confined to the older areas of a town or city and they tend to be narrower, shorter and older than roads. Like an aged, wizened and shrunken person, they are filled with history, quirks, strange happenings and puzzles. To walk down a street is to walk with the past, to hark at the cries that once went on there, to smell the odours that once lay heavily hereabouts, to feel the textures that once hung around, to see the sights that once were drawn here and to cant with those that once lived nearby. Alleys, entries and passageways, too, are intriguing, leading as they do almost mysteriously from one place to another but yet having a life of their own. Too small to impact on a wider area, such little throughways draw us into a highly localised world, dragging us away from the global to the day-to-day life of a specific and small place.

Too often in our redevelopments, streets, alleys, entries and passageways have been erased from history - and with them has gone not only the look of the past but also the feel of the past. Fortunately, Wolverhampton retains a number of these captivating places, many of which have a distinctive local name – fold. Throughout the Black Country, the word fode is used for a yard. Derived from the term sheep fold it continued to have a vitality in the urban and industrial setting generations after its original meaning had been swept away with the rural scene. And today, the folds of Wolverhampton call back to the beginnings of the city as a major centre of the woollen trade. Diligently, enthusiastically and sympathetically, Anthony Perry has delved into the history of Wolverhampton through the folds of the city. In doing so he brings from the mists of the past into the glare of history people long dead, events long forgotten and trades long gone. This is a remarkable work by a man who is infused with a love of his City and with a passion for bringing its story into the present and future. It reaches back successfully into the Middle Ages and bonds the city of the twenty-first century with its roots. Most of all, The Folds of Wolverhampton is a tribute to those who lived, worked, played, laughed and cried in the heart of one of England's great urban centres.

This book is dedicated to my late Grandfather, Francis Weetman, a self taught scholar. His life-long love of books and the knowledge they could provide instilled in me a similar enthusiasm, resulting in a long journey of discovery researching local history.

CHAPTER *1*
INTRODUCTION

Cities, towns and villages all over the country have their access-ways between buildings, at the backs of buildings, at the sides of buildings, which are not regarded as "streets" or "thoroughfares" in the accepted sense of the words. Maybe they are too narrow for vehicles to use, and are therefore no more than footways. Maybe vehicles can enter at one end but not exit at the other, if there is no way out at all, if that way out is blocked by bollards or it becomes too narrow to be any more than a footway. These access-ways may be un-named. If they do have names, a variety of titles can be found – passage, row, court. Some places use their own particular words, such as shuts and scuts.

We lived in Red Lion Street in the middle of Wolverhampton in the 1950s, and the lower end of Paternoster Row opened out on to the street, but not for vehicles. The families in the street did not refer to it as Paternoster Row – it was just "the alley". There was a low brick wall with railings set into it and an opening in the middle, about the right width to have had a gate hung, and a step down on to the pavement. The opening always seemed to be large enough for the ball to bounce out on to the street, just at the right time for a car to have to brake, and then we children would have to mutter "sorry" to an annoyed driver.

The intention of this book is to take a look at those alleys, passages and little streets in the centre of Wolverhampton that bear the name "fold", and a few others which could quite easily have also borne the title, because of their nature. In doing so we shall see what points of interest and bits of history we can discover, and think about whether they may have any connections with the wool trade, with which the town was associated in Mediaeval times, before industries to do with metal grew and became predominant. We can do this by following a circular route, starting and finishing in Wulfruna Street, between the Civic Centre and the main University buildings.

1

CHAPTER 2
THE WOOL TRADE

The title of "fold" seems to have become popular in the central part of Wolverhampton – what was really the full extent of the town before it expanded during the nineteenth century – and is still in use in several places today. Whilst this may have had its origins in the wool trade, who can say if these "folds" were actually used for gathering sheep together?

What we do know is that the wool trade in the Middle Ages made Wolverhampton prosperous, as it did many towns around the country. It held a high position among the industries of England from the 12th century right through to the 19th century. From the beginning of this period, everywhere there was an organised weaving industry with gilds of weavers in the larger towns and citics.

The woollen industry began to decline in the early 14th Century, and the numbers of skilled artisans dwindled. Edward II tried to prop up the trade by prohibiting the import of foreign cloth. Edward III took steps to rekindle the trade by encouraging skilled craftsmen, from Flanders and Brabant in Belgium, and Zeeland in the Netherlands, to settle in England and pass on their skills to English workers. There were also some restrictions on the exporting of woollen yarns, and on the importing of foreign cloth.

The Black Death was a major setback, both as to the horrific devastation of life, and to the alienating of craftsmen. As wave after wave of the plague arrived in England from Europe and the East, towards the end of 1348, possibly half the country perished. Maybe Wolverhampton was not so badly affected. Writing in 1686, Dr Robert Plot said,

"From which scarcity of waters and high situation it is, that not withstanding the adjacent Cole-mines they enjoy a more setled health than most of their Neighbors, as breathing a more subtile and refined Air…….. Whence perhaps it comes to pass, that the Plague has scarce ever been known in this place, but the smallpox frequently, both signes of salubrity……"

The alienation of craftsmen, much reduced in numbers, but on whom great restrictions were imposed in plying their trade, led to the Peasants' Revolt in 1381, and unrest which continued for many years. Whatever the local effects, there was a period of recovery, and by the early 15th Century the wool and cloth trade was playing a big part in increasing Wolverhampton's prosperity. The wool would come from the sheep districts around England and on the Welsh borders to towns such as Wolverhampton, where it would be spun into yarn, then woven into cloth.

Many leading families were trading in wool, and there were important citizens who were members of the Staple of Calais. The Staple was a fixed place through which exports had to be directed, and the staplers were a company of merchants who dealt with the wool that passed through it. Calais had been seized by Edward III in 1347, and was English territory. Toward the end of the century the Staple was settled in Calais, which had good access to the merchants of Flanders, and this lasted for about 200 years. However, in 1617 the export of wool abroad was abolished, together with the foreign Staple. 20 home staples were set up, and merchants were allowed to buy wool anywhere in England, and sell it in any staple. Without foreign trade, the staplers tried to get into the cloth trade, but found themselves in conflict with the clothiers.

Whilst the roads of this time were poor in assisting communication and trade, the River Severn was the great highway through the Midlands. From Saxon times one of the main roads out of Wolverhampton was the route to Bridgnorth, itself a town which had a wool trade. Low Town around the river crossing developed in mediaeval times as a port, which continued to be of importance until the 19th century and the coming of the railways. It would therefore seem likely that here was the Wolverhampton traders' link their markets.

The types of traders could therefore be divided into:

1) The staplers, or Merchants of the Staple, who would buy and sell the raw wool, and arrange for its export. The Society of Staplers was the oldest corporation of merchants in English trade abroad.

2) The clothiers or drapers, who would be responsible for all the processes, from picking the wool, combing, washing, spinning and weaving, to fulling, dying and finishing, so manufacturing the woollen cloth to sell it to the tailors. They might buy the raw material, and make the profit from the sale of the finished article, so there would be tradespeople to carry on the different processes in between. Blackwell Hall in London was the national place for marketing of goods by clothiers. This contained separate halls for use by different counties or localities.

The process of spinning was generally done by women and children, perhaps outside, or in a spinning room reserved in a house. The work would take up any leisure time people had. Weavers would work for hire on woollen yarn supplied by the clothier, to make cloth of a given size. They would work at home, and be paid for their labour when the job was done. Wool-combers were in a superior position. Their numbers were limited, their work demanded a lot of skill, and they were not necessarily tied to a particular place. The cloth finishers were also known as cloth-workers, cloth-dressers, shearmen or croppers. They were generally employed in a workshop rather than at home. Scribbling was another term used, for preparatory carding, in order to separate the wool fibres.

This trade was to continue in the town for a long time to come, as can be seen from the following names which appear in records:

Nicholas Ridley, Merchant of the Staple of Calais, 1504
John Nechells, Merchant of the Staple, died 1531
James Leveson, Merchant of the Staple, died 1547
Richard Creswell of Barnhurst, Merchant of the Staple, died 1559
John Leveson, Merchant of the Staple of Calais, died 1575
Thomas Offley, Merchant of the Staple of Calais, died 1580

Thomas Leveson, Merchant of the Staple 1567, died 1594

John Cresswell, Merchant of the Staple 1587, died 1593

Henry Planckney, Merchant of the Staple 1582-7, died 1608

Richard Creswell of Barnhurst, Merchant of the Staple 1592, died 1612

Thomas Huntbach, "mercator stapelie", died 1624

William Waring, Clothier, will dated 1444

John Howlett, Draper, from 1534

William Creswell, Clothier, died 1560

John Gough, Draper, died 1597

Robert Cutt, Draper, 1560, died 1599

Henry Gough, Draper, 1602, died 1656

John Hanbury, Draper, died 1636

Graseley Old Hall was the property of Nicholas Ridley. Nearby house The Lea, from which we now have the name Lea Road, was owned by the Waring family. John Nechells left to the town land at Greenfields, the income from which was to pay for the repair of the town's roads. The name Greenfield Lane still exists, although a lot of the land has been built on. The record of his bequest is not contained within any Deed, but is set out on a plaque on the wall above the font in St Peter's Collegiate Church. John Nechells was son-in-law to another local man who became wealthy through the cloth trade and a benefactor, Stephen Jenyns. He became a Master of the Company of Merchant Taylors, and after serving as Alderman and Sheriff, was Mayor of the City of London in 1508-9. He was knighted by Henry VIII in June 1509. He founded Wolverhampton Grammar School in 1512, purchased the manor of Rushock, Worcestershire, to finance the maintenance of a schoolmaster and usher, and left the care and government of the school to the Merchant Taylors Company. Three of the "houses" into which boys were divided were named Jenyns, Nechells and Offley. Such was the wealth of Sir Stephen Jenyns that he paid substantially for the reconstruction of the church of St Andrew Undershaft, Leadenhall Street, in the City of London in the 1520s. His coat of arms, together with the arms of The Merchant Taylors Company, are carved on the front of the gallery in St Peter's Church. This gallery was constructed in 1610 by the Worshipful Company of Merchant Taylors in London for the use of the Grammar School boys.

Perhaps the traders who had grown wealthy by the early 15th century felt they wanted to make their mark, for Christian or for their own reasons, and considered the style or condition of St Peter's Church was unworthy of a prosperous town. Certainly they were the ones who paid for the remodelling and part reconstruction, which included for the lowering of the north and south aisles, raising the nave on new columns to take a clerestory, and building a new tower on the Early English arches at the central crossing point. The work began in 1439 and continued through the century, to create the grand place of worship which is, apart from the chancel, broadly similar to the Grade 1 Listed building we see today.

Trade Directories begin to be available towards the end of the 18th Century, by which time it would be expected that Wolverhampton, becoming industrialised, would have lost its connections with its earlier successful business. But remnants of the trades can be found. For instance, the 1770 Directory reveals 1 flaxdealer, 2 hosiers, 12 mercers or drapers, 2 woolstaplers and 1 worstedmaker and comber. Elizabeth Calcott in Cock Street (Victoria Street) was listed as being both a hosier and a woolstapler. The 1792 Directory similarly shows people still involved in the industry, with 1 dyer, 3 flax dressers, 1 silk dyer, a woollen manufacturer, 2 woolcombers, a wool dealer, a wool stapler, and the same Elizabeth Calcott in Cock Street described as a worsted seller.

Although the effects of the Industrial Revolution were obviously seen by 1817, William Pitt, writing his book on Staffordshire at that time, was still telling his readers that the town was surrounded by gardens, and that the air was generally healthy.

CHAPTER *3*
WADHAM'S FOLD

This is the newest of all the Folds, as it was only created after 1978 when the Civic Centre was completed. It runs down a slope from the St Peter's Square end of Wulfruna Street to the pedestrianised part of North Street, and is no more than a paved footway.

The name Wadham's recalls a street lost as a result of the construction of the Ring Road in the 1960s and 1970s. Wadham's Hill descended about 35 feet (11 metres) in height from its junction with North Street, where there was a large area used for parking in front of the Molineux Hotel, and where a row of houses was actually called Molineux Fold, down to a traffic light controlled crossroads with Waterloo Road and a tree-lined Bath Road. The line of the street was in existence in 1750, as can be seen from Isaac Taylor's map of the town surveyed that year, although it was the bank itself on this map that was called Wadham's Hill. But who was Wadham?

In 1817 William Pitt mentioned that there was an ancient arched well at Waddam's-hill, called Meg-a-doodle's-well, but by then it was neglected.

The present Wadham's Fold runs down over the site of the old Wholesale Market, and what was the lower end of Wulfruna Street, where it joined North Street. This route happens to cross the site of another Fold, "Best's Fold", part of a larger area

Cottages in Wadham's Hill, dating from the middle of the 19th century, looking down towards the turn into Red Lion Street, and the junction of Waterloo Road at the bottom. The photograph must have been taken towards the end of their life in the 1960s. (Photograph courtesy of Wolverhampton Archives and Local Studies.)

An excellent aerial photograph, taken in May 1935. From left to right, we see Wadham's Hill, St Peter and St Paul's Church, Paternoster Row, the former Bluecoat School, with the block of four houses in Red Lion Street where the author lived in the second house from the right, the new Telephone Exchange next to Mitre Fold, and with Jessup's and the Old Mitre Hotels still at the top of the Fold. Then we see the site of the Civic Hall, the Town Hall and the rooftops of Blossom's Fold just beyond. The retail market hall is centrally placed, just below St Peter's Collegiate Church, and the open market patch and wholesale market cover the site of Best's Fold. (Photograph courtesy of Wolverhampton Archives and Local Studies reproduced with kind permission of Simmons Aerofilms.)

which the Council purchased in February 1877. The vendor was Thomas Bayley, Rates Collector. At that time Horse Fair was a dog-leg street partly along the route of Wulfruna Street, and Best's Fold was a large collection of houses, public houses and other buildings around a yard which led off North Street. So the land assembly created the opportunity for the Council to provide an open market, or "market patch", so that the outside stalls could be moved from Cheapside. It also created the site for a wholesale market hall.

The name Best undoubtedly harks back to Richard Best, builder of the former Deanery House, which stood where the main University entrance building is now. He acquired the land in 1656, then built the hall in the style of Sir Christopher Wren. As the great architect's father and uncle were both Deans of Wolverhampton and Windsor, it is possible he was responsible for its

design. This was part of the case put forward for its preservation, but to no avail, and the Technical College was built on the site.

A modern view of the most modern of Folds, looking down the path towards Giffard House. (Photograph Joyce Perry.)

CHAPTER *4*
PATERNOSTER ROW

Almost opposite the foot of Wadham's Fold is Paternoster Row, now just a street, with the large 1960s and 1970s telephone exchange on the left-hand side. But on the right are links with the old "alley" which we looked at in the introduction. At the top, fronting North Street, is Giffard House, a fine, early Georgian House, believed to have been designed by the Warwick architect Francis Smith, and built between 1727 and 1733. It was purpose built as a public mass-house and priest's residence, and is therefore the oldest Catholic church, as against being a private chapel, in the country, which has been in continuous use since it was built. The sanctuary of the church is the original public chapel. Some of the original furniture bought for the house may still be in use.

In the early days Catholics met for "prayers", as saying Mass in public was not allowed. The Catholic Relief Act of 1778 stopped penalties for saying Mass, and in 1791 Catholics were permitted to register chapels for public worship.

Modern view of St Peter and St Paul's Catholic Church and Giffard House in Paternoster Row. (Photograph Joyce Perry.)

This emancipation led to existing chapels being registered and new ones being built.

Giffard House became headquarters of the Midland District, and in 1804 John Milner became Vicar Apostolic. He was one of the great figures in the history of the Catholic Church, and when he died in 1826 it was decided he should be buried in the orchard behind Giffard House. The Church owned quite a tract of land, going right down to Red Lion Street. It was also decided the church

All of St Peter and St Paul's Church was hidden from view in North Street, and Giffard House was partly hidden, by the collection of older buildings with their arched entrance into the Chapel Yard. The 1820s houses are on the right of the picture. (Photograph courtesy of Wolverhampton Archives and Local Studies.)

should be extended over Bishop Milner's resting place, as a memorial, by building a new nave and two transepts on to what already existed. What we see now is the building designed by architect Joseph Ireland in a Grecian style, completely restored in 1989-90 at a cost of one and a quarter million pounds, with an appeal fund and grants from English Heritage and the Council. New statues of St Peter and St Paul repeat what had been part of the original design, and railings were later added to the Paternoster Row boundary.

Catholic ownership covered lands to the north and south of the church buildings too. To the north was a group of small houses, turning the corner into Wadham's Hill. To the south, three rows of houses stood, side on to North Street, one of these being Paternoster Row. Between the first and second rows the space was named Chapel Yard with, opposite the steps to the church entrance, a further row of three slightly larger houses with the name Bishop's Place – recalling Bishop Milner, no doubt, and dating from his time.

I remember these in existence when we lived in Red Lion Street in the 1950s. Chapel Yard, renamed Paternoster Row, was our "alley",

Two of the 1820s houses at the top of Paternoster Row, opposite the entrance to St Peter and St Paul's Church. The gates opened into the church school playground. (Photograph courtesy of Wolverhampton Archives and Local Studies.)

leading down the hill to the walled burial ground, consecrated in 1828 and still there today. As children we were warned against climbing over the wall to play in the very overgrown cemetery. When our voices could be heard in there, parents would call out: "Come out of there, or you'll catch the fever."

Red Lion Street was less than half its present width until 1926, when the Council purchased various plots of land from the Catholic Church to widen the highway and develop three blocks of four houses and one pair of semi-detached. These were to be let to tenants, who included firemen and policemen employed at the stations in buildings which now form the back part of the Magistrates' Court buildings, or old Town Hall. These houses had very little in the way of gardens, some with none at the front at all.

We lived at No. 2, which with No. 3 lost some of the already shallow rear garden to old toilets of the former Bluecoat School, which had become education offices and a children's dental clinic – memories of nightmares having gas for tooth extractions! We were among the first tenants to be moved out in the Autumn of 1962, so that the telephone exchange could be extended, over the site of Numbers 1 – 4, with the offer of only one alternative house to which we could move. No compensation for disturbance or home loss was given then, as people can thankfully claim these days when they are moved out of their properties by the Council. So marked the end of a happy few years in a street with "the gang", and the advantages of being so close to the town.

Was Paternoster Row ever a "Fold"? The 1750 map shows an unnamed lane or passage leading away from the back of Giffard House down to Green Hill Walk, between marked out gardens or produce growing sections of ground. Beyond Green Hill Walk was the Little Broad Meadow, which may have been used for pasture, and Giffard House fronted on to one of the main streets of the mediaeval town. Maybe the lane was used for driving animals up to that street, but there were other more suitable routes.

Chapel Yard, off North Street, perhaps in the 1920s, showing demolition of late 18th or early 19th century houses which later became Paternoster Row. The gables of the Bluecoat School, later Educational Offices and Dental Clinic, can be seen in the background. (Photograph courtesy of Wolverhampton Archives and Local Studies.)

A modern view of the grand early 18th century frontage of Giffard House. (Photograph Joyce Perry.)

A modern view of the Church of St Peter and St Paul on Paternoster Row, backing on to Giffard House, with the statues of the two saints above the entrance. (Photograph Joyce Perry.)

CHAPTER *5*
MITRE FOLD

The former name for North Street was Goat or Tup Street, and this may be our first link with the wool trade. The word tup, meaning a male sheep or ram, was in use from the 13th Century, and perhaps a sheep market was sited here. We shall see that street names may change for definite reasons, or there may be alternative names that are interchangeable.

Just a short walk along Red Lion Street, past the 1960s telephone exchange extension and the older exchange building, will bring you to an ordinary-looking street with the name Mitre Fold. This became ordinary through the Council widening it, after purchasing properties on both sides of a narrow access-way, between 9 and 10 feet (3 metres) wide, which had steps at its Red Lion Street end, to prevent it being a through route for vehicles. Walking up the hill back to North Street it is difficult to imagine it being that narrow.

It is amusing to think that the two establishments which sat just 3 yards (metres) away from each other, either side of the Fold at the North Street entrance, were a licensed hotel and a temperance hotel. The licensed premises was

called "Jessop's", purchased by the Council from Atkinson's Brewery in 1926 for £15,532 – 14s – 0d. This was then leased out to Butler's of Springfield Brewery on a 3 year agreement at a rent of £200 per annum, including its brewhouse, malthouse,

Modern view of Mitre Fold. (Photograph Joyce Perry.)

stable and other outhouses, but excluding half of the site, which extended down to Red Lion Street and was simply marked as a garden on the plan.

Why only half the site? The alcoholic and non-alcoholic establishments still stood either side of the narrow Fold, so in leasing them out the Council were not ready to demolish and make way to widen the Fold. But there was an intention to carry out improvements, and the first was to widen Red Lion Street at the bottom of the hill to its current width, and to build some Council houses. The half that was not let would correspond with the site of the oldest part of the telephone exchange, so perhaps the opportunity was taken to make a start on this. After 'Jessop's' was demolished, the land on which the 1970s telephone exchange stands formed the site of a wooden Citizens' Advice Bureau, with a garden where commemorative floral displays would be planted. For example in 1969 there was one to celebrate 125 years of the YMCA.

The other property was the "Old Mitre", perhaps because a Catholic Bishop lived not many yards away and which we can assume gave the derivation of the name of the Fold, and this was sold to the Council by Violette Amy Jullien, wife of Raoul Jullien, of Poule, Rhone, France, for £2,550. Did the difference in price for the two establishments reflect that this one was unlicensed? The conveyance mentions that the temperance hotel had previously been a public house, and the sale included the cottages 2 – 16 Mitre Fold, which were all small, with outhouses in a shallow communal rear yard reached by one central entry. These cottages almost reached the Red Lion Street end, and, although they fronted Mitre Fold the deed refers to them as having been erected in Mitre Yard.

The 1750 map shows the route of Mitre Fold, with the name Mill Alley, as far as the steps we have mentioned, before it turned to the left then at an angle arrived at Green Hill Walk (Red Lion Street) – perhaps because of the difference in levels. This map also shows possibly the inn and the first few cottages. Why Mill Alley? There is no evidence of a mill being there. Name changes and alternative

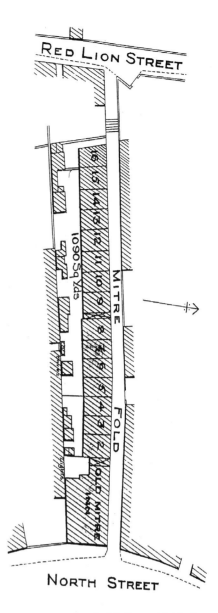

Plan from conveyance dated 26 June 1919 from Violette Amy Jullien to the Council, of the Old Mitre Inn and cottages in Mitre Fold. (Courtesy Wolverhampton City Council.)

names were not uncommon. But water was not necessary for a mill. In 1817 it was recorded that in the town there were several steam-engines, working various mills, one of which was upon a large scale, for the spinning of woollen yarn for carpets.

By 1827 the whole row of cottages were there, and the name was Mitre Fold. The 1871 town map shows the Fold ending in steps down to Red Lion Street, still narrow. Because the lower end of the Fold was not straightforward and even narrower, it would be very difficult to use it for animals, but if Tup Street was so named for the reason that it was used for a sheep market in early

A corner of the grand Victorian market hall on the left and the gates to the Education Offices, formerly the Bluecoat School, on the right, frame this probably 1930s view of North Street. In the centre the Old Mitre Hotel and Jessup's Hotel stand either side of the narrow Mitre Fold. The gabled building further along the street was originally the Monmore Prebend House.(Photograph courtesy of Wolverhampton Archives and Local Studies.)

days, then the upper part of the Fold, before the cottages were built, could have been convenient for the temporary penning of animals pending their showing and sale.

The "Old Mitre" was let by the Council, to be used strictly as a temperance hotel, the tenant in 1925 being Ann Taylor from Leigh, near Stoke-on-Trent, paying a rent of £35–5s–0d. The schedule of fixtures shows it was still fitted with gas brackets and pendants, and there were venetian shades and roller blinds. Instead of bars, guests had the option of the sitting room and the bagatelle room, and for refreshment there was the restaurant as well as a coffee room.

Next to the "Old Mitre", set back from North Street, was a Georgian house which had been in use as the town telephone exchange. It was to be several years before the site between Mitre Fold and Corporation Street was to be redeveloped by the Council with the new Civic and Wulfrun Halls, designed by Lyons and Israel in the style of the Stockholm Concert Hall and built between 1936 and 1938.

Also within this site was one of the Prebend Houses of St Peter's, that of Monmore. From the time of Lady Wulfrun, St Peter's, or the Minster of St Mary as it was originally dedicated, was run by a Dean and several Prebendaries or Priests, who had responsibility for each district or village under the control of the main church. Each had a Prebend house in the town. Across the street stood the house of the Prebend of Willenhall. With other Prebend houses and church property around the space between St Peter's Church and North Street, it could be regarded in the same way as a "cathedral close". The significance of this aside to our subject we shall see shortly.

Although not a property within a Fold, but associated with the cloth trade, across the street it is interesting to note that within the block between Cheapside and Queen Square was described in a Lease and Release dated June 1722 "a dwellinghouse in Goat Street alias Tup Street, with four lower rooms (shop, kitchen, washhouse, pantry) four chambers above, and two garrets over the chambers, a cellar under the shop, a stable, and a building used as a dyeing house".

CHAPTER *6*
BLOSSOM'S FOLD

If we move along North Street we come to the Town Hall, now the Magistrates' Court but, until 1978, when the Civic Centre was completed, the main Council offices. Built in 1869-1871 in a French Renaissance style, the grand entrance hall still contains the statue of George Benjamin Thorneycroft (1791-1851), the town's first Mayor when it became incorporated in 1848.

This was the site of the Lion or Red Lion Inn, after which the street was renamed, from being Green Hill Walk, as the Inn Yard with its stables and outhouses stretched down to the narrow street at the bottom. Here began the work of the Town Commissioners, who ran the town before there was a Council. It was recorded that on Friday 30th May 1777 12 men "assembled at the dwelling house of Thomas Badger, known by the name and sign of the Red Lion Inn."

The Council bought this establishment in July 1858 from William Tarratt and John Shaw, merchants, and the Wolverhampton and Staffordshire Banking Company, and converted it for use as its main offices. The Council is noted as having already started to use the property, and indeed the plan on the deed shows Town Clerk's Office, Borough Surveyor's Office, Rate Collector's Office and Accountant Clerk's Office. The document referred back to a lease and release in 1833, to which various persons were party, including the Most Noble William Harry, Duke of Cleveland, the Right Honourable Henry Vane, Earl of Darlington and the Right Honourable Lord William Powlett. Here we see where names of some of our streets came from. Also involved was Richard Evans, coach proprietor, who borrowed upwards of seven thousand pounds from the Bank. The property was described as the Lion Inn with coach-houses and stables, and a right of carriage and horse road thirty feet wide from the back gates of the Inn yard into a new street called Darlington Street. The converted Inn lasted until Councillor Henry Hartley Fowler led the proposal to have a new Town Hall built on the same site, grand enough for the status of the town. The width of the new development left enough space on the cleared site to lay out Corporation Street.

Next to the Red Lion, and also purchased by the Council in 1859 to make way for the new Town Hall, was a property described as a copyhold messuage or tenement and garden in North Street formerly called Tup Street or Goat Street, late in the occupation of Elizabeth Cobbe and Mary Anne Mitton, and a malthouse late in the occupation of William Walker and a warehouse lately in the occupation of William Alderton, and three other dwellings, all of which had been converted into one property occupied by Elizabeth Mitton and somebody Atkins (no first name given). Also involved in the deed were several noble personages, as with the site of the Town Hall, and the sale to the Council was from Thomas Freshfield Scarth of Staindrop, Durham and the Most Noble Henry Duke of Cleveland. It referred to a lease and release in 1809, being a settlement on the marriage of Henry Duke of Cleveland, then Viscount Barnard, with Lady Sophia Powlett. Henry Duke of Cleveland as Lord of the Manor of the Prebend of Wobaston agreed to take £235 for the enfranchisement and sale of the copyhold

interest. A second document refers to the Court Baron for the Manor of the Prebend of Wobaston in May 1804 in which William Mitton, maltster (father of Elizabeth Cobbe, née Mitton, and Mary Ann Mitton), was admitted to the copyhold property, to hold for ever, at the will of the Lord, by yearly rents, heriots, customs and services due. William Mitton left the property in his will to his wife with money for the daughters' upbringing. The Court Baron in 1827 admitted Elizabeth and Mary Ann to the copyhold property to hold for ever in coparcenary at the will of the Lord. The property was then released to Mary Ann Mitton, who was then seised in fee simple according to the custom of the Manor of the Prebend of Wobaston of a good and sure lawful and indefeasible customary estate in fee simple.

A maltster is someone involved in brewing ale, literally, in making malt by allowing grain to be

Modern view of Blossom's Fold. (Photograph Joyce Perry.)

steeped in water to sprout and to dry it in a kiln. The legal terms may need explaining. Whereas fee simple is an unconditional inheritance, a copyhold interest is the right to hold land according to the custom of the Manor, by a copy of the roll made by the steward of the Lord's Court. A copercenary is a joint heir to an undivided property, and heriot is a fine due to the Lord of the Manor on the death of a tenant, originally his or her best beast or chattel.

The side of this property abutted Blossom's Fold. We have already looked at the subject of Prebend houses, and now we have the site of another, that of the Prebend of Wobaston. Two of the Prebendaries of Wobaston in the 14th Century were named "de Blastom" or "de Blaston", and legal documents in 1609 refer to the Prebend house lying between Tup Street and Blassoms Foulde". So here we have the derivation of the name and some indication of an age for our next Fold.

The 1750 map shows it as Blossoms Court, with a narrower opening into Tup Street, a wider space at the dog-leg left turn, then a dog-leg right turn where the opening is now into Darlington Street, to join up with the end of Green Hill Walk. From that corner Crooked Alley followed the slope down towards Chapel Ash. The 1802 compilation of trades and professions in the town by local eminent historian John Roper is taken from the town Rate Book. It gives a useful insight into the kind of employment people had at the time, and their various locations. Only one person is listed under Blossom's Fold, Simon Lansdale, a keymaker, at No. 6. Smart's 1827 Trade Directory map shows the name Blossom's Fold.

There is a date plaque of 1874 on the Town Hall Hotel (Little Civic) at the corner of North Street. The deeds of this property show it was sold to Wolverhampton and Dudley Breweries in 1902 by Reverend Richard Weston of Burntwood, William Henry Hill of Claverley and Archer Benjamin Smith. It had been rebuilt as the Town Hall Hotel in 1874 following the enlarging of the site in 1871. The White Lion stood on the corner,

The old frontage of "The Tiger", now Kipps, in North Street. (Photograph courtesy of Wolverhampton Archives and Local Studies.)

and next to it were a dwellinghouse and a fruit warehouse occupied by a Mrs Hoccom, George Holt and their tenants. Readers may recall that many years ago Kipps Wine Bar was know as the Tiger, and the 1960s frontage hides an older property. These properties were also part of the Wobaston Prebend, and it was in 1857 that the Ecclesiastical Commissioners released their reversionary interest. Deeds in 1833 refer to the White Lion and the Tyger.

The 1871 town map shows on the same site the public house and maybe another couple of small cottages of similar size to those at the corner of the left-hand dog-leg which were until recently occupied by commercial estate agents Michael Tromans and Company. This firm had preserved these former cottages, with a new roof and rendering outside. Inside the small rooms were converted into office accommodation. They back on to Age Concern café and premises and the shops which form, with the covered entrance, a continuous frontage to Darlington Street, and from the architectural style and age of materials must date at least to the making of that street. However, the rear part of Age Concern shows evidence of pre-dating the frontage, by its difference in height of floors, barrel vault in the cellar, and the 1871 map shows this rear part was separately occupied from the front. Look above the side door to see two wide windows, modern replacements of possibly early windows made wide to allow more light for work purposes.

It was recorded in 1838, by a Mr Lewis, one of the Town Commissioners, that "the Commissioners had prosecuted a suit against a Mr Thrustans, to compel him to take down an archway and rooms in the centre of a range of buildings he had erected over the carriageway leading from North Street, through Blossom's Fold, to Darlington Street. They compelled Mr Thrustans to cut through a large mass of new building the whole way to the roof, laying it open to the heavens. Some time later one of their friends purchased the adjoining house and had permission from the Commissioners to re-erect the building Mr Thrustans was compelled to pull down. I was present at the meeting when consent was given to rebuild and I then protested against it, not only as a "job" but as a monstrous injustice against Mr Thrustans." However, the minutes record only the final permission to build in 1835. This story may give us a date for the middle section over the entrance to the Fold – looking up at this, it would appear it could have been re-erected separately to what is on either side. As to the first date of building, this might have been years before, as similar stories of archways and obstructions being ordered to be removed by the Commissioners related to structures which were

already many years old. Also the story shows that the Town Commissioners, who were in power from 1777 until the town was incorporated in 1848, were not responsible to anyone and represented no one except themselves.

The proposal for the new Darlington Street was made in 1814 by the Town Commissioners, but it was not finally constructed and opened until 1823. There was the question of culverting the watercourse shown on the 1750 map, the Puddle Brook, or Black Brook as it had become known, but the main delay was caused by Mr Evans, the innkeeper of the Red Lion, objecting. The Inn yard led out across Green Hill Walk into Red Lion Walk (leading down to Chapel Ash) which was owned by Evans' own landlord, Lord Darlington. His land, which covered much of the area needed, had not been included in the Compulsory Purchase special Act of Parliament, because he had already agreed to sell to the Commissioners and to wait for his money, hence the naming of the street after him. So the scheme was delayed until Mr Evans retired. In acquiring property for the new street, Commissioner Moreton was requested to make a valuation of the property in Blossom's Fold of a Mr Mitton, which property had been offered for £841. It was finally purchased for £742. Shortly afterwards notice was given to 11 tenants of houses adjoining the Fold included in the property purchased. Perhaps these were the section of the Fold which fronted on to the right hand dog-leg where it stood in the way of the new street.

The next property around the dog-leg from the site of the Prebend House was bought by the Council in 1902, from Reverend Richard Weston of Burntwood and William Henry Hill of Claverley. They derived their right to sell from being Trustees of Mary Ann Smith of Farewell near Lichfield, and Joseph Crowther Smith. On the plan the cottages opposite are also shown to be held by the Trustees. Considering its position it is curious that the powers quoted in the conveyance of the property, section 34 of the Wolverhampton Improvement Act 1869, refer to property needed for "widening or enlarging or

The Queen's Hotel at the corner of North St and Cheapside, taken perhaps in the 1930s, is instantly recognisable despite several name changes in recent years. The words "Empire Palace" can be seen on the back wall of the stage of the Hippodrome which was burnt down in 1956. (Photograph courtesy of Wolverhampton Archives and Local Studies.)

rendering more commodious any street or otherwise for the improvement of the Borough." It must have been quite new, as it was not shown on the 1871 map, but had been built by the 1880s. A few years ago it was altered and had its frontage made more fitting to its age for the Electoral Registration Office to move in. Before then it had been occupied for many years by Age Concern, who ten years ago moved into the building at the corner of the Fold and Darlington Street, and backing on to the cottages.

The next buildings may, like those opposite, have been here since the opening of Darlington Street or before. Trisha's has been in business, dealing in "vintage" style clothing, for 30 years. A link with the 1960s and a claim to have a local celebrity is that her husband Giorgio was a member of the group Freddie and the Dreamers, amongst other bands. The property contains a blocked "gothic" window showing evidence of its history. Look above the shop to see the line of the former pitched roof. Trisha and Giorgio believe this was removed in Victorian times when the property was converted from a cottage to a shop. Next door still has an early style of windows, perhaps showing it pre-dated Darlington Street, with stairs up to the Electrolysis Centre and Just Nails. The changes in floor levels to these areas are quite complex. On the ground floor, wrapped around the corner of Darlington Street under the covered entrance to the Fold, with its late Victorian or Edwardian style windows, is a bistro café, latterly Vincent's, which had become hugely popular for its individual range of foods, now under new management.

CHAPTER 7
TOWNWELL FOLD

The 1750 town map shows that, after turning the right-hand dog-leg of Blossoms Court, within a short distance on your left would be the entrance to a narrow lane, roughly where the present entrance is to Townwell Fold. Going down this lane on your left would be the gardens of properties fronting Cock Street (Victoria Street), and on your right would be the Cock Bowling Green. The Cock Inn, which gave its name to the street, was one of the long established inns of the town, dating at least to the early 16th century, when it was sold to James, one of the wealthy Leveson family who grew important through the wool trade. It was burnt down in the great fire of 1590 and rebuilt. By 1770 it was being called the "Cock and Bell".

Having set the scene, we can look to Dr Robert Plot, writing his Natural History of Staffordshire in 1686, to find the origin of our next Fold. He notes that Wolverhampton, "being situate high and where they have but four weak springs to supply that large town, which too rise all together behind the Cock-Inn (so that they may be esteemed but as one) having different names appropriated to their respective uses, as the Pudding-well, the Horse-

well, the Washing-well, and the Meat-well, from which last they fetch all the water they use for meat or drink all over the town in great leather budgets or boraccias laid cross a horse with a tunnel at the top whereby to fill them, such as they use much in Spain, and some other towns in England, as York, Worcester & c. bringing to the other three, their tripes, horses and linnen."

At the time of the Town Commissioners, Wolverhampton was still split into two Manors, the Deanery and Stowheath, both of which used the same wells. The duties of the Constables appointed by the Manors therefore included the repair and cleansing of the town wells.

The 1750 narrow lane ended abruptly at a row of buildings and the entrance to a small, enclosed field, Cock Close, along the southern side of which was a feature called "The Tenters" – rows of hooked supports on which cloth was hung for stretching after processing. Here is the origin of the saying "on tenterhooks". The Puddle Brook is shown next to "The Tenters", and forming one boundary of the Cock Close. Is it not feasible these features were located near to each

Two modern views of the top section of Townwell Fold. (Photographs Joyce Perry.)

other for a purpose? The brook and the Linen-well were available for clean water, the close for keeping animals at the end of the "fold", and one of the recognised places for stretching cloth near to buildings which may have had something to do with processes in the wool industry. This use may have disappeared quickly from the location, because the 1802 list of trades and professions shows eleven persons carrying on different industrial trades at addresses in Townwell Fold. Only three have connections with animal skins – James Heath at No. 5 and Thomas Ward at No. 10, both curriers, and John Taunton at No. 7, a tanner. A currier was someone who dressed and coloured leather, which had already been tanned, i.e. made into leather from the raw hide by soaking in liquid that contains tannic acid. Doubtless they had some kind of connection, being so close. The others are:

No. 9 - William Watts, Boxironmaker
No. 12 - Thomas Titterton, Hingemaker
No. 13 - Joseph Harley, Toymaker
No. 14 - Thomas Kirkmore, Locksmith
No. 15 - B Hopkins, Brazier
No. 16 - Isaac Green, Cabinet Maker
No. 17 - Robert Owen, Cabinet Maker

However, there is a remnant of the cloth trade in the description of No. 6 as a "weaving shop", where Aaron Ironmonger traded as a ropier.

By 1827 the town map in Smart's Directory shows Townwell Fold following a snake-like route, from two entrances in Darlington Street, with an exit into Cock Street (Victoria Street), in the position where Skinner Street was to be constructed thirty years later, then down to an exit on to Salop Street, close to its corner with Worcester Street.

The 1842 tithe map shows something similar, but the southern section of Townwell Fold is omitted from the map.

Skinner Street was built in 1861 and is shown on the 1870 map connecting Victoria Street (renamed after the Queen's visit in 1866) and School Street. Skinner Street was so called because of a skin and hide business – remember the trades in Townwell Fold in 1802? Townwell Fold, with its yards, passages and various buildings, followed the same route it used until Beatties' 1958 extensions meant it had to be diverted underneath their five storey high new building. Until then the fold crossed Skinner Street where Victoria Passage comes out now. Then it disappeared around the back of properties fronting the lower section of Victoria Street, before it reached the exit into Salop Street.

This 1950s route is the one our gang in Red Lion Street used to run down to the Saturday Matinee film show at the grand Odeon, thankfully now a listed building for its typical 1937 Odeon style, designed by Harry Weedon for Oscar Deutsch, owner of the chain of cinemas. Here we were regulars for the children's programme, which others will no doubt remember included a cartoon, "cliff-hanger serial" and a main feature. We were thrown out for something fairly innocent like flicking pellets at each other, and told not to darken their doors again. Of course they would not remember us after a while. The intervening period was spent at matinees at the ABC Savoy, from which we were turned out for swearing at usherettes, before returning to the Odeon.

In Victoria Street the Cock Inn survived in part until the 1920s. A little further up the street there was also the old Giffard Arms, whose back yard opened into the Fold.

James Beattie opened his first shop in 1877, known as The Victoria Drapery Supply Stores and this became successful and expanded.

In 1911 the building which now houses the toy department at basement level was built by Manders

Back-to-back cottages and cobbled yard in Townwell Fold in 1913, looking towards the back of Victoria Street properties. Near to the position of the photographer were outside toilets shared by the householders. This part of the Fold was soon to be redeveloped for commercial uses. The demolition men who have stopped for the photographer are being watched keenly by a small boy outside the end cottage. (Photograph courtesy of Wolverhampton Archives and Local Studies.)

Paints and Varnishes as an extension to their operations in St John Street. Beatties bought this in 1931 and opened the store extension five years later. James Beattie had passed away on 31st May 1934. Beatties bought the building on the corner of the existing entrance to the Fold which had been Jeanette's Gown Shop in about 1960, about the same time as they acquired the frontage next door which had been Bradford's Store. The second entrance to the Fold in Darlington Street, whose position can be estimated at the back of properties where the Fold does a right turn, disappeared as the street was completely built up. The lower section of the Fold is clearly marked on the 1919

The first James Beattie and his family. (Photograph Joyce Perry courtesy James Beattie plc.)

The newly completed Victoria Street façade of Beatties after the 1929 rebuilding showing the crescent and entrance to the arcade which led to Townwell Fold. (Photograph Joyce Perry courtesy James Beattie plc.)

The back fold or alley known as Giffard Arms Yard, running from Victoria Street to Townwell Fold, in the 1920s, before the properties were to be rebuilt, following the widening of Victoria Street. A washing line stretches across between the Inn's stable block and the Gentlemen's toilet with its lamp hung conveniently outside.
(Photograph courtesy of Wolverhampton Archives and Local Studies.)

Ordnance Survey, with many cottages, outbuildings and business uses, and two exits into Salop Street.

Drastic changes to both northern and southern sections were to happen within a few years. In 1929 the Council decided the upper part of Victoria Street, between Skinner Street and Queen Square, needed to be widened by about fifteen feet, which involved demolition of all the properties on the western side. Whilst this did of course mean the loss of some fine and interesting buildings, as can be seen in old photographs, it also resulted in the complete frontage we have today, including the wonderful façade of Beatties with its arched windows and concave curve, where there was originally an arcade leading through to Townwell Fold. This arcade lasted from the 1929 reconstruction until it was taken out in 1955. The rear entrance to it was filled in, and built up to three storeys in 1965, as can be seen from the newer brickwork next to

the former Mander's building. The stationery and confectionery section of the ground floor of the store is in what is left of the former Picture House cinema, hence the different floor levels, and the pitched roof of the cinema part can still be seen from the windows to the stairway above.

This cinema was built at the rear of a club fronting Victoria Street in 1911, and so had a narrow entrance for its patrons. It continued to show films after Beatties bought it in 1925, but closed just as the "talkies" were arriving in 1929, the same time as the widening of Victoria Street was to lead to such wholesale reconstruction.

My mother worked at the store in her teens, and could therefore remember these changes. She was also there early enough to remember the first James Beattie as an "old Father Time" character, a kindly person who was appreciative of his staff. His grandson James Beattie, who died in 1987, was also well liked by my mother's colleagues during her time there, and he threw a party for them to celebrate his twenty first birthday.

The 1929 redevelopment created a modern type of fold, Victoria Passage, at the rear of the new Victoria Street premises, with warehouses fronting on to the other side. The end building at the corner of Victoria Passage dates from 1926, and this was the premises of Ward and Son, electrical and heating engineers. This was bought by Beatties in 1960.

At the corner with Skinner Street was a pleasant 1930 building of Mander's Paints, which Beatties purchased in 1953, using land around it for staff parking. It was finally demolished in order to extend the surface car park in 1970.

With the reduced size plot at the junction of Skinner Street with Victoria Street in 1929, the land was sold to Hortons' Estate Ltd of Birmingham, a family commercial investment company, to build a parade of shops with offices above, still part of the complete façade of the period, with an entrance hall also of the same period.

Part of the land developed by Hortons was the site of 49-53 Victoria Street and 1-5 Skinner Street, purchased by the Council in 1912 from Thomas Brownsort Banks. The deeds of these properties go back to 1803, when local builder Moses Anslow bought from surgeon George Perks and others a house, storehouse and warehouse in Boblake, near "Pinson's Gutter". Additional properties were: a barn converted into a warehouse and workshop, and a stable and workshop. All the property was described as being situated "at or near certain Spring Wells or Fountains commonly called the Town Wells." Also included in the collection acquired by Thomas Banks, and sold on to the Council, was property described as follows: "all those shops or buildings heretofore used by Messrs Millington and Smith as Painting Shops and Bellows Shops and which were previously 5 small messuages or dwellinghouses at or near ... the TOWN WELLS ... being part of the hereditaments formerly erected on the site of 5 bays of barning

formerly the property of James Perry (Merchant) and also formerly copyhold of inheritance within the Manor of Wobaston" and land "on part of which there was a Town Wall". Was this just a mistake in spelling, or does it signify something else? Having referred to *the* Town Wells, would it have then said for the latter piece of land that there had been *another* Town Well? Previous writers have said the former name of Cock Street, Tunwalle Street, was just a minor change from Town Well. However, the Anglo-Saxon word for a well or spring was "wyllan", whereas the word for wall was "wealle".

William Pitt in 1817 said that the town was for many years supplied with water from these wells by the water-works erected by Dr Wilkes, which had been long discontinued, and that a plentiful supply was by 1817 being obtained from numerous wells sunk a considerable depth through the solid rock upon which the town was built.

Aside from giving us a rough idea of the site of the wells, we also learn that properties in Victoria Street and Skinner Street were copyhold of Wobaston Prebendal Manor. These were enfranchised in 1875.

Ward's 1926 building in Townwell Fold, which runs to the left of the building before rising up the slope towards Darlington Street. Ward's building, now a part of Beatties, can still be seen next to their new extension. Victoria Passage now runs to the right, and was created when Victoria Street frontage properties were rebuilt in the 1920s. (Photograph courtesy of Wolverhampton Archives and Local Studies.)

CHAPTER 8
VICTORIA FOLD

We mentioned earlier that the 1750 plan showed a passageway following the route of Townwell Fold at its top end, leading to some buildings, Cock Close and the Tenters. It also showed an entrance from Cock Street into a yard of buildings where Skinner Street is now, and another yard of buildings at the southern end of the Fold, where it emerged into Salop Street. This expanded greatly over the next 150 years, but the shape of the yard and buildings was generally still there on the 1870 map and indeed a remnant of it in 1919, not many years before the area was to be cleared.

Modern view of Victoria Fold. (Photograph Joyce Perry.)

The Council decided that the lower part of Victoria Street should be widened too, by just a few feet, as should also Skinner Street, School Street and Salop Street. So the whole block was due for demolition of its buildings fine, and those not so fine, to judge from the cramped conditions of the cottages in Townwell Fold. There had also been a beerhouse called the Bee Hive, and the hide and skin market – remember the tanner and two curriers in 1802?

Hortons' Estate Ltd were by 1935 owners of a number of properties in the block. The Council owned a limited amount of property, but agreed an exchange with Hortons, to acquire from them as much land as possible in front of the new road improvement line. This took place that year. One of the properties involved was the former public house known as the "Golden Lion", at the corner of Townwell Fold with Salop Street. This property, which included a brewhouse at the back, was built over the Fold at first floor level, and had a separate cellar. It was sold in 1887 by Thomas Charles Cooper to W Butler and Company. The Council bought this from Butlers' Brewery in 1935, then sold it on to Hortons. One of Butlers' mortgagees was Henry Ernest Fowler, Second Viscount Wolverhampton, son of Sir Henry Hartley Fowler. He signed the documents with the one word necessary – Wolverhampton.

The exchange of lands did of course mean Hortons were able to build the two-storey row of 1930s shops in Victoria Street and turning the corners into Skinner Street and Salop Street, now protected as part of the Worcester Street Conservation Area. These retain much of their original character, although there are a few modern intrusions to the shopfronts and windows above. Hortons' scheme also replaced the lower Townwell Fold with Victoria Fold. This is a private road, but it does provide an access to business premises, as well as garages and rear servicing. This modern "Fold" was not completed, around the back of the Odeon, until the 1960s, when the shopping parade around its western side was developed, with frontages to Salop Street, School Street and Skinner Street.

A modern view of the entrance to Victoria Fold in Skinner Street, with the tower of the new Market Square dominating the skyline. (Photograph Joyce Perry.)

A row of typical 17th or 18th century cottages fronting Skinner Street, but before the street was built in 1861 this was the middle section of Townwell Fold, and now where Victoria Fold is situated. Note the privacy shutters to the lower part of the front living-room windows. What might the two ladies, and the one gentleman in the doorway, have been thinking about the reason for someone taking their photograph? (Photograph courtesy of Wolverhampton Archives and Local Studies.)

CHAPTER *9*
FOLD STREET

Just a short distance down Salop Street we come to the entrance of this ordinary and unassuming little thoroughfare. As it bears the name "Fold", however, we will stop and consider if it has any relevance. It appeared as a dog-leg street on the 1871 map, linking Salop Street and School Street. The lower extension of it at the back of Staffordshire Building Society is modern. Until the 1960's, School Street Council Depot bordered the northern side of the street.

If we go back in time we see that maps in 1842 and 1850 showed an opening off Salop Street, roughly in the same place as Fold Street is now, next to the New Inn. Of course these maps do not say what was behind the frontage. However, the New Inn itself is a comparatively modern replacement of an old "New Inn". This was on a smaller site, as the corner of Fold Street was occupied by two shops, 108 and 109 Salop Street. These were sold to Wolverhampton and Dudley Breweries in 1935. The Brewery, in the names of Henry and John Banks, which is why we say Banks's Brewery, purchased the old inn for £575 in 1885 from a Mr John Hipwood. The site was L-shaped, in that it went around the rear of the two

Modern view of Fold Street. (Photograph Joyce Perry.)

26

A deserted lower end of Salop Street, looking up towards the turns into Art Street, Brooke Street and Fold Street on the left, Peel Street on the right. Some of these properties would have undoubtedly survived the name change from Barns Street. (Photograph courtesy of Wolverhampton Archives and Local Studies.)

shops. Mr Hipwood had bought it ten years earlier from Joseph Broadbent, William Richardson and his wife Ann Matilda, when it was described as the New Inn and brewhouse, shops, stable yard and two sitting places in pew 103 in the north aisle of the Collegiate Church. Because the older documents do not contain plans or detailed descriptions of the position of property, it is not clear whether the inn, or the shops referred to, replaced houses – there are so many documents to marry up, and the older ones are sometimes difficult to decipher.

A lease in 1780 shows the period when a street name change was taking place, as it refers to the address as being in Barn Street or Salop Street. This document is between William Wright, bucklemaker and Phillip Mullender, breeches maker. A link with the wool associated trades is found with perhaps the father of

William Wright. Thomas Wright, a locksmith, leased property to Samuel Cale of Willenhall, weaver, for one year. The document is dated the 23rd January "in the 24th year of the reign of our Sovereign Lord George the Second" - 1751. The rent was "one peppercorn to be paid upon the feast of St Michael the Archangel," i.e. the Quarter Day, 29th September.

The 1750 map shows in this location a small enclosure fronting Salop Street with built up development on each side. Could the enclosure have been used for keeping animals, and could the street have been named on the basis that some kind of "fold" was here? After all, Salop Street's old name of Barns Street was based on the type of buildings there. In addition to houses, there were barns and stables, and hay, corn and straw stacks in this street, as we discover from reports of two great fires in 1590 and 1696.

A picture postcard entitled "Old Houses Salop Street, Wolverhampton". Making allowance for artistic licence, the turn into Peel Street can be seen on the left, the spire of St Mark's above the roof tops, and the building on the far right would be the "New Inn" before the late Victorian re-building. (Photograph courtesy of Wolverhampton Archives and Local Studies.)

A 1950s view of the predecessor to the present "New Inn" in Salop Street, with the corner of Fold Street on the left. The 1920s shops next door still survive on the set-back building line. The snow covered car park at the corner of School Street was to be developed with a 1960s shopping parade.

(Photograph courtesy of Wolverhampton Archives and Local Studies, with permission of Jim Dowdall and Wolverhampton Photographic Society.)

CHAPTER *10*
BENNETT'S FOLD

This is a name that has recently disappeared, with the development of a large retail and residential block, with its distinctive landmark tower and stone-fronted colonnade to the ground floor shops. This faces a new Market Square, with the new buildings having been developed by William Kendrick and Sons on land leased to them by the Council, and in conjunction with Kings Oak, who are responsible for the flats on the upper floors. Kendricks also developed the Square itself for the Council, as a new open-air market.

The name "Bennett's Fold" was last seen fixed to the wall of the alleyway at the side of the building which Capital Cookers occupied for many years, before moving into the new unit. So, to walk along the front of the new building is to walk along a part of the route of the Fold. Capital Cookers' old property, on which they had invested much in refurbishing, hid a remnant of another former inn, the Angel, the age of which could not be determined. Much alteration had taken place many years ago, and before Capital Cookers it had been used for a long time as a furniture shop.

Modern view of the new Market Square which replaced Bennett's Fold. The arcade of arches follows the same line. (Photograph Joyce Perry.)

We have already mentioned the agricultural nature of buildings in the old Barn Street. The 1750 map shows the south side of the street was quite built-up. Peel Street, on the western side of the retail market halls, was then an undeveloped

A snowy scene in Bennett's Fold. The cottages on the right back on to Worcester Street properties. The gabled building at the end fronts Salop Street and survives in a changed form. (Photograph courtesy of Wolverhampton Archives and Local Studies.)

street with the name Brickhill Alley, and Pitt Street, a 1960s change of name from Great Brickhill Street, was Brickhill Lane – a brickkiln is marked on the map. The space between Barn Street and Brickhill Lane was made up of gardens and growing areas and a harp-shaped close or small meadow. This almost reached across to a yard area with buildings that could have been a forerunner of Bennett's Fold. This suggests that there was always the possibility of uses connected with animals, but nothing is certain.

Properties on the west side of Worcester Street were copyhold of the Manor of the Prebend of Wobaston. In 1777 John Dickin, victualler, had copyhold property at or near Sawyer's Gate and at the top of and fronting to Brickkiln Lane. In 1782 Joshua Devey, Thomas Sherratt, Joseph Austin and Mary Butler surrendered into the hands of the lords of Wobaston Manor "seven messuages or tenements in Milstone Street but now commonly called Worcester Street with a Court Yard and two Shops Brewhouse and Garden thereto adjoyning...and bounded by buildings late John Dickin's...on the South-west." If Millstone Street was the former name for

Worcester Street, perhaps Sawyer's Gate was a term used for the area behind, which was to become Bennett's Fold.

The block became known as the Brickkiln Patch, and was heavily developed over the next hundred years, with Bennett's Fold meeting at right angles a street called Brickkiln Croft, and many small courts off them, with cottages and business uses. The area was cleared by the Council, with the aid of an unfit housing Compulsory Purchase Order made in 1931, when it was said safety was such that policemen would only walk through in pairs. Amongst properties bought by the Council were No. 6 Bennett's Fold, described as house, builder's yard and stores; No. 18 was a house with blacksmith's shop; Nos. 18½, 18a, 20, 21 and 22 comprised five houses, two workshops, stables and coalyard. These tell of a mix of uses.

A few industrial uses remained, and the new Retail Market was opened in 1960, to replace the grand Victorian Market Hall in North Street. The Pitt Street car park was enlarged in the late 1980s when the remaining backland property of Bennett's Fold was purchased by the Council and cleared.

Where does the name come from? Bennett in mediaeval times was spelt in various ways, and is supposed to derive from Benedict. But, bearing in mind that there were a lot of courts off Salop Street which are just numbered on plans, without names, it may be that the simple explanation is someone locally gave the name through usage. For instance in 1802 there were two Bennetts, both locksmiths, in property on the northern and southern sides of the "Patch" – Edward at Court No. 8, Salop Street, and Thomas at 41 Brickiln Street.

CHAPTER *11*
CLEVELAND PASSAGE

From the site of Bennett's Fold, we move up Salop Street and across the traffic lights into Cleveland Street. Behind the first buildings on the left we arrive at a fairly ordinary accessway to the backs of properties fronting Victoria Street, and the backs of some very 1960s-looking 1960s shops which front Cleveland Street and Bell Street on the other side. But it does bear a name, which relates to the street it leads off.

If we take a look at the 1750 map this shows no Passage or street of any kind. Development along the eastern side of Boblake continued south into Worcester Street, and those properties which faced down Barns Street had small yards and garden areas at the rear. Further south along Worcester Street, probably the only building from this time to remain with us today is the "Plough and Harrow" public house. The shape of this suggests a timber-framed structure, with perhaps a jettied first floor originally. Here we have remnants of the houses of the Prebendal Manor or Lordship of Kinvaston. This consisted of: "houses on the East side of Worcester Street, including the 'Queen's Head' going down nearly to the Penn Road, house and shopping at the corner of Cleveland Street and property some distance also towards Penn, being a range of twelve houses, five other houses in Worcester Street and two houses fronting Cleveland Street, also three other houses in Cleveland Street".

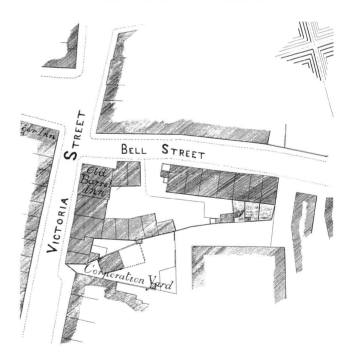

Plan showing layout of buildings at corner of Victoria Street and Bell Street, including Old Barrel Inn, until redeveloped by Council in 1876. (Courtesy Wolverhampton City Council.)

In 1817 St Peter's Church is recorded as being serviced by seven Prebends, in addition to the Dean and Sacrist, the Prebend for Kinvaston being Reverend Peter Thoroton. The 1839-43 ledger of rents received from occupiers of Kinvaston Manor properties includes a detailed map of the street. This shows two corner buildings at the recently constructed junction with Cleveland Street. Beyond these, along Worcester Street, there is a mixture of buildings which were to be replaced in a few years with what we have now. However, the "Plough and Harrow" public house was excluded from the Manor holdings, and the shops on the site between the public house and Temple Street show some similarity in shape to that of the very much altered three storey shops we have today.

On the 1750 map there appear to be no properties fronting Boblake at all of the same shape as those there now, but the shape of the block is not dissimilar. However, the former block seems to have been built a few feet further forward than the buildings there today.

Bell Street in 1750 had two alternative names – Belcroft Street and Hollow Lane. Where Cleveland Passage is now the plan shows, fronting Belcroft Street, four narrow strip gardens, and, to the left of and behind these, an L-shaped area, which, although not marked, has symbols across it like the brickkilns on other areas on the map. If this part was used for brick-making, the part beyond, which extended as far as Grea Pea Walk (Temple Street), was still used for agricultural purposes, being marked as M. Bretts Close. Strip fields adjoin this Close and extend up to Snow Hill. The Close has a boundary on Grea Pea Walk but also has two passageways leading to it from Boblake and Worcester Street, i.e. off one of the main thoroughfares of the mediaeval town.

We have another survival of the woollen trade on the other side of Belcroft Street, where there are more Tenters shown. Gardens separate these from Belcroft Street, but a narrow space along the full length of the northern side of the Tenters ends in a right-angled turn into an access-way on

Bell Street, near the junction with Victoria Street, about 1960. The decorative building on the corner is still there, backing onto Cleveland Passage, with the start of a new shop building next to it, replacing Bell Ironworks. The lettering "Iron Fencing" is above the tall window. (Photograph courtesy of Wolverhampton Archives and Local Studies.)

to Belcroft Street. Who used the Tenters? Were they based in Belcroft Street? Did the wool come from Mr Brett's Close?

Cleveland Street was developed from 1828, followed by Cleveland Road, creating a through route from the west to Bilston Road without having to negotiate the narrow streets in the middle of the town. It was not the Town Commissioners who developed the route, but the Duke of Cleveland, the former Lord Darlington. Hence the name.

The 1827 Smart's Trade Directory map shows nothing of Cleveland Street, therefore. It does show Bell Street instead of the two older alternative names, and it also shows Worcester Street being used as the name for Boblake, as far the corner of Bell Street. This is borne out by the 1802 Trade Directory, in which Boblake is not mentioned. But the 1842 Tithe Map persists in using the old name. Perhaps it continued to be used locally. By 1842 much of the frontage of Cleveland Street had been developed, including properties on the corner of Boblake and Worcester Street, the buildings we see today. The one on the corner of Boblake was known as the Old Mitre Hotel. Empty now for many years, and before that used as a shop, the upper floors show little alteration inside or outside. Note the blind windows upstairs to avoid paying window tax. This unpopular levy was first introduced in 1696, and increased six times between 1747 and 1808. It was reduced in 1823, and repealed in 1851. There was a standard sum to be paid on any small house, but a sharp increase for properties with ten or more windows.

The 1842 map does not show the full depth of buildings where blocks are built up and do not contain open pieces of land. So Mr Brett's Close had gone by then, and most likely the Tenters, as the northern side of Bell Street was developed. However, a long, shallow building is shown fronting on to Bell Street, to the rear of the Boblake frontage. When we see the 1870 town plan, which does depict all buildings quite accurately, this identifies the long, shallow building as a terrace of individual, small properties, behind which was a yard with more small buildings, which also backed on to properties fronting Victoria Street, as it was now renamed. These properties jut out into Victoria Street, and the whole collection stops

Cleveland Passage from getting to Bell Street at its present point of exit. The rest of the Passage, however, is there as it is today, with a dog-leg to avoid the collection of property. The buildings backing on to the Passage are all set back to their position today, and all appear to be the same as those we have today, save for the more modern middle property with its false second floor frontage.

The collection of buildings at the corner of Bell Street in 1870 was destined not to survive much longer. Using its powers under the Wolverhampton Improvement Act 1869, the Council purchased them all in 1876, as part of a scheme to regularise the width of Victoria Street and to widen Bell Street – by a few feet – it must have been such an important highway that it needed widening!

The smaller purchase of four dwellings in Bell Street by the Council, for the sum of £750, was from Sarah Beddoes, John Cooper, John Beddoes, William Cartwright Beddoes and William Donnelly. The sale refers back to the Will of John

The other Mitre Hotel in the 1960s. An imposing 1830s corner house at the junction of Victoria Street and Cleveland Street, backing on to Cleveland Passage. It still stands, empty for many years, awaiting rescue, its upper floors inside and outside showing little sign of modernisation. (Photograph courtesy of Wolverhampton Archives and Local Studies.)

The "Old Barrel Inn" at the corner of Victoria Street and Bell Street about 1870. The landlord's name J.Bee features on the sign. Perhaps he is the one standing apart from the others posing for the picture. You can see the degree to which the buildings beyond, which are mostly still standing, are set back, with the widening of Victoria Street. (Photograph courtesy of Wolverhampton Archives and Local Studies.)

Cooper, father of the one seller, in 1832, when the houses were occupied by Joseph Parker, Mary Legg, Samuel Amos and George Copage. The 1802 Rate Book includes a Legg at Bell Street - who was a watch chain maker.

The larger purchase, from John Cooper on his own, for the sum of £3,650, was of three properties in Bell Street, occupied at the time of the sale in 1876 by Henry Watkin, Benjamin Hatherley, with one void, five properties in a street formerly called Worcester Street, but now known as Victoria Street, which were occupied by Joseph Bee, John Bason, Joseph Howlett, Richard Dudley and Stephen Davis, two more properties fronting Bell Street occupied by Thomas Kinley and Joseph Bee, and five more properties with stables at the back of Bell Street occupied by Joseph Howlett, Thomas Haddock, John Bason, Thomas Lister, Sarah Leek and Joseph Bee.

The building at the corner of Victoria Street and Bell Street was the timber-framed "Old Barrel Inn", its landlord being Joseph Bee. Why did this survive the great fires in the late 16th and late 17th centuries, along with 19 Victoria Street (Lindy Loo)? The 1750 map shows the Puddle Brook stopping just short of Boblake, somewhere between Belcroft Street and John Street. This brook was most likely open across the street and up Belcroft Street, hence its alternative name Hollow Lane. So here was a small source of water to extinguish fire. The presence of the brook would also explain why the Tenters were sited here, and why John Street had a dog-leg at the bottom of its slope, because a natural feature made it easier to turn towards the main thoroughfare.

Along the rest of the Victoria Street frontage in 1876 properties were much the same as now, with the exception of the middle shop, with its false second floor front. Many years ago this was the premises of Timothy White's, until taken over by Boots.

Next to the row of properties purchased in 1876 the Council already owned a triangular shaped piece of ground, used as a Corporation depot. The whole section of land, once cleared of buildings to widen the street, was sold in plots, so we have a date for the buildings we see now, all built as one in the same style. Some of the original features survive, including the fine decoration under the eaves, oriel bay window at first floor and decorative brickwork. The corner plot was sold to Joseph Bee, whose new building was a public house named the "Old Barrel Inn"! He bought the corner plot for £1000, and plot 4 for £570. The middle plots were sold to the former tenant Mr Bason for £930.

At this point Cleveland Passage assumed its current straight route, and the rest of the land the Council owned was sold to the next-door industrial owner, Mr Butler, for £510. The 1885 Ordnance Survey shows the factory fronting Bell Street as Bell Works (Iron), and the one fronting Cleveland Street as Cleveland Works (Safe and Lock).

The shops fronting both streets date from the 1960s. Before they were built there was a plan to build a modern style shopping arcade running through between the streets which would perhaps have been more suitable.

The whole area to the east of here is due to undergo a vast transformation in the next few years. This will be the biggest redevelopment seen in the centre of Wolverhampton since the Mander Centre and Wulfrun Centre in the 1960's. The Council has selected a Dutch company, Amstelland NV and Multi Development Corporation NV, known as AM Developments UK Ltd, who have a high profile track record of exciting city centre developments throughout Europe. AM's design will see the restoration of historically and architecturally important Victoria Street and Worcester Street frontage properties in the Conservation Area, to give them back a full economic life, combined with a new development all the way up Cleveland Street to Snow Hill. The new part will be a mix of traditional and modern buildings, in an open pedestrian street style, linked with a series of public squares and spaces. A

A view, perhaps from the late 19th century, looking at a row of typical 18th century three storey cottages on the south side of Bell Street. (Photograph courtesy of Wolverhampton Archives and Local Studies.)

department store, shopping, leisure uses and apartments are intended to revitalise this part of the City Centre. It is hoped the many businesses affected will be able to relocate in the scheme or nearby, with the minimum of disruption, and not have to move further afield.

At the heart of the site is Summer Row. It was only forty years ago that this became the wide, featureless link between two streets that it is now. Summer Row is also the name given to the accessway between properties fronting Cleveland Street and Temple Street, and here is a pointer to its early history.

Look at the 1750 map again, and we see nothing more than Mr Brett's Close, with an open entrance between fences fronting Grey Pea Walk, and a row of trees forming an eastern boundary to three fields or closes.

Look at the 1842 Tithe Map, and we see buildings fronting much of the new Cleveland Street, with a "National School" on the south side. This was an attractive design by architect Ebbels, built on land given by the banker Alexander Hordern, and opened as a Church of England

A modern view of the 1876 buildings at the corner of Victoria Street and Bell Street which back on to Cleveland Passage and stand waiting for a restoration scheme. (Photograph Joyce Perry.)

School in 1832. Next to the school on the map is a narrow strip of land with, on its eastern side, an alley with buildings which has a right angled bend to a long cul-de-sac behind Cleveland Street property. By the time of the 1871 map the alley has a long narrow building on its western side, but with a distinct strip of land between alley and building. This ties in with a lease dated May 1863 between Edward Griffin, former Wolverhampton merchant, who was now styled "gentleman", of Towersey Manor, Buckinghamshire, and George Hughes, hingemaker. Within 1757 square yards fronting Temple Street were stables, sheds, and the land was bounded by a ditch adjoining Summer Row. The cul-de-sac appears to be home to back-to-back and other cottages.

By the time of the first Ordnance Survey in the 1880s, the narrow strip has gone, and the land on the western side of Summer Row is more heavily developed with Temple Works (Ship Building Fittings) and a Meeting Room of the Plymouth Brethren, now part of All Nations Church. In April 1894 the site was sold by James Whitehouse Griffin of Towersey to Francis William Yates of The Wood, Codsall Wood, but it is still let to George Hughes as a manufactory, stables and sheds.

A modern view looking up Cleveland Passage from Bell Street. The trees showing over the walls are a result of neglect to empty properties in Victoria Street. (Photograph Joyce Perry.)

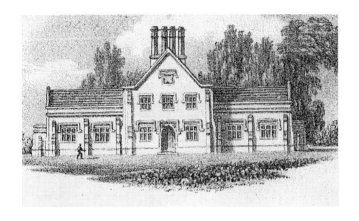

The National School, Cleveland Street, 1833 (Picture courtesy Wolverhampton Archives and Local Studies.)

No. 2 Summer Row, Wolverhampton.

The Birthplace of
REV. JABEZ TUNNICLIFF,
Founder of the First Band of Hope.
Born 1st Feb., 1808.

Birthplace of Reverend Jabez Tunnicliff, 2 Summer Row (Picture courtesy Wolverhampton Archives and Local Studies.)

For the Griffin family origin, we need to look at the deeds for the land at the rear, the site of what was 32 Cleveland Street. These documents start in 1779, but in 1833 William Duffield, maltser, had recently erected a building on the site fronting the new street, then called Cleveland Road. It backed on to Summer Row, which was in the ownership of a Mrs Walker. To the east was prebendal land of Alexander Hordern, in the occupation of a Mr Griffin and used by him as a Rope-Walk. This is perhaps the reason for the narrow strip of open land between Cleveland Street and Temple Street, and for the ditch. A rope walk would have been a long, narrow shed or alley used for the spinning or twisting of rope.

We can confirm Summer Row was in existence many years before Cleveland Street, as in 1808 it was the birthplace of a man destined to found one of the great Christian organisations for children. No. 2 Summer Row, as can be seen in the photograph from a postcard, was a small two-storey cottage. Here was born Jabez Tunnicliff on 1st February 1808. He became a Church Minister and in 1847, with 72 year old Ann Jane Carlile from Ireland, formed the Band of Hope, to promote Christian teaching for children and help them avoid the problems of alcohol. As the movement spread rapidly, "signing the pledge" was a feature of meetings throughout the country and abroad, where a commitment was made to abstain from strong drink. They made good use of the magic lantern as a teaching aid, and old glass slides used at meetings can still be found and are shown by lanternists operating period-style shows. Hope UK is the modern successor to the Band of Hope, providing education for children on the avoidance of alcohol and drug abuse.

Summer Row was privately owned, and was at least partly laid out before Cleveland Street was constructed. As for its name, it is possible to read too much into things, but the word did mean a pack-horse, and also a summer is a horizontal bearing beam or lintel, especially for the support of roof joists or rafters - maybe there is a connection with what was on the site?

CHAPTER *12*
FARMER'S FOLD

We move a little way up Victoria Street, past the three oldest buildings which remain in the street – the timber-framed No. 19, then No. 18, the left-hand side of which was rebuilt a few years ago in 18th century style to replace a modern intrusion, and No. 17 which still has its 18th century first and second floor façades.

We come to a 1960s building with a passageway at the side which leads past some small shops into the Mander Centre. Farmer's Fold sounds like a made-up name, making use of the idea of the town's agricultural past, but we will see what historical facts we can confirm about it.

We have already seen that the 1750 map does not give the names of all the folds, courts and alleys. Whilst Farmer's Fold is not named, by comparing its position with more modern maps, we can see that its route is marked, from Cock Street, through a narrow opening, along a passage with a long narrow range of buildings, then a slight bend to the right between a garden on the left-hand side and a small building to the right. The passage then borders the back yard of a row of buildings which front John Street, before emerging into that street, near to where the old 1712 Grammar School buildings stood.

The 1827 Smart's Trade Directory and 1842 Tithe maps show the passageway similarly.

We have to remember the plans of different periods may have different styles of showing features. So, whereas the 1750 map does not show arched entrances into streets and folds, but leaves gaps between buildings, the 1870 town map does not show arched entrances at all, thus making all look like solid buildings. This happens where the entrance into the Fold near the turn in John Street goes under a continuous row of buildings. After crossing a bit of open yard the Fold follows a similar route as on the 1750 map, with a similar range of small buildings on both sides. There is a continuous run on the southern side, and on the north a range of property with varying frontage lines. The exit into Victoria Street is down a narrow passage between two buildings. The First Edition Ordnance Survey in 1889 shows the same arrangement but in more detail, and the name Farmer's Fold is marked.

1955 photograph of 16 and 16a Victoria Street with the entrance to Farmer's Fold to the left, and the shop front of Povey's bakery and restaurant. (Photograph Joyce Perry, reproduced by kind permission of John Bayliss.)

In June 1894 a conveyance of the property between Arthur Henry Marindin, Francis John Dalbert and Joseph Northwood describes the whole as "messuage tenement or dwellinghouse situate in Cock Street …..with the warerooms several cottages stable coach house outbuildings and appurtenances thereto belonging situate on the right side of the yard known as Batches Yard there passing from Cock Street to John Street and which said yard called Batches Yard lies behind the messuage in Cock Street … formerly in the occupation of B Crockett and his undertenants AND ALSO ALL THAT Malt House with the Pump and other appurtenances formerly in the occupation of W Wright also a Yard formerly called the Walled Garden with Coachhouse and Privy all which said Malthouse pump yard garden cottages house stable and privy are on the left hand side of Batches Yard … formerly in the occupation of George Copage …"

Joseph Northwood died in 1915, and his widow Rebecca and daughter Laura Maud Elizabeth sold the whole property to J and W Povey Ltd, for £2700, who were already trading from the front in Victoria Street. By this time the description goes as follows: "….shops warehouses cottages and premises known as 16 and 16a Victoria Street….and also the site of Farmer's Fold……together with an area of land containing 334 square yards….and the 8 cottages and outbuildings thereto.…"

So we have two alternative names for the Fold, and a trading name, Povey, which is in use today. Povey's was probably like the Copper Kettle which traded in the Lindy Lou building – a well-loved tea-room, with dining-rooms on the first and second floors, and a bakery and confectionery shop on the ground floor.

To deal with the name Farmer first, we have to look at old Council deeds relating to property at the eastern end of King Street, backing on to Wheeler's Fold, and fronting Princess Street (previously this was known as Berry Street). In 1751 Thomas Evans, carpenter and joiner, sold some land for building new property on King Street, which had just been laid out, to George Foxley, brassfounder. Between 1754 and 1757 Mr Foxley entered into four mortgages or charges in favour of Edward Farmer, and borrowed the sums of £100, £80, £20 and £30. Edward Farmer was a baker, and the Fold was named after him. He was a subscriber to the publishing of the Sermons of Reverend Benjamin Clement, headmaster of Wolverhampton Grammar School and first Minister of St John's Church – the Sermons were published in 1769-1770, after the Minister's death. The property off Cock Street had been previously known as Bache's Fold, so the name had stuck. Presumably a descendant, another Edward Farmer, is recorded as operating as a baker in the Lindy Lou building in 1818. His address of 19 Cock Street was joint with Benjamin Best Farmer, Excise Officer. Benjamin was still living there in 1827, but perhaps Edward had passed on by then, for Mary Farmer is listed as being "baker and flour-dealer".

So what of the name Bache? The Bache family were prominent ironmasters in the 18th century, and it was recorded that William Bache of Wolverhampton fixed the first steam engine to raise any quantity of water at Wolverhampton in March 1712. Perhaps because he died in August the same year this prevented any great recognition for his achievement. The statement "William Bache, gentleman gave 12 pound towards casting us 1698" appeared on bell number nine in St Peter's Church. His father, Thomas Bache, was churchwarden in 1683, and he died in 1695. He was of the Bache family at Penn, and he was one of the trustees of money left by Reverend Charles Winn, or Wynne, to "be disposed of for the poor of Penn and to set them to School and buy them Bibles".

On the left-hand side of the Fold, Waterstone's Bookshop, previously Dillon's, was preceded by Waring and Gillow's furniture shop. But older readers will remember the traditional drapery emporium of Bedford Williams, where the giving of change to customers made for a fascinating experience. The bill written by the serving assistant

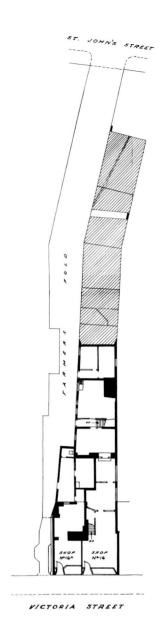

Plan of 16 and 16a Victoria Street from 1955 sales details, showing premises of Povey's and buildings in Farmer's Fold. (Courtesy of John Bayliss.)

and the money tendered would be tucked into a small metal canister which would then be placed into a vacuum tube system running around the store. So the canister would disappear for a few minutes, before returning with the bill receipted and your change, as if by magic. Who was the responsible clerk at the other end, checking the money?

There was a sale of property to Arthur Bedford Williams in 1931, and he was succeeded by Norman Bedford Williams, who sold it to the company called Bedford Williams Ltd in 1958. Was

The lower part of John Street in the late 1800s showing the eastern entrance into Farmer's Fold and some typically local eighteenth century cottages. (Photograph courtesy of Wolverhampton Archives and Local Studies.)

Looking between the half demolished infill panels to the timber frame structure of Farmer's Fold cottages, to catch a glimpse of Bedford Williams' window display, 1955. (Photograph courtesy of Wolverhampton Archives and Local Studies.)

this the whole family business story? The Company sold to the Council bits of the building that jutted out to enable the width of the Fold to be regularised, and in 1961 a Janet Snow, as employee of the Company, had to make a declaration to confirm they had used the property for 40 years as a drapery. So here you could say there was a 20th century link between the Fold and the cloth trade!

In 1954 J and W Povey Ltd put up for auction the property described as 16 and 16a Victoria Street, along with Farmer's Fold. As can be seen from the photograph in the auction particulars it was a three storey 18th century building, two windows on the second floor being blocked in and indicating someone having to take account of window tax, with the entrance to the Fold under the adjoining building.

No. 16a was let to Ashley United Industries Ltd, and trading as Brighter Homes, presumably

Advertising the Farmer's Fold shops at the John Street end in the 1960s. Bedford Williams' side entrance is on the right. (Photograph courtesy of Wolverhampton Archives and Local Studies.)

Cottages in Farmer's Fold, taken in 1955 looking towards the back of the three storey building in which Povey's Bakery and Restaurant was housed. The hooded flue pipe rises out of the Restaurant's first floor kitchen area.
(Photograph taken by, and reproduced with permission of Jim Dowdall, Wolverhampton Photographic Society.)

A modern view looking down Farmer's Fold towards the entrance from Victoria Street, showing the distinctive first floor design above the end shops. (Photograph Joyce Perry.)

some kind of home decorating supplier. No. 16 was to close, but up to that time had been Povey's, bakers, confectioners and restaurant. The staircase from inside the shop led to a restaurant, coffee room, kitchen and preparation area on the first floor, and a further two dining rooms and small kitchen area on the second floor.

The range of buildings which lined the Fold then was put to rather uninteresting uses – offices, garages, and a two storey building which had been stables, but were now just store rooms.

The property was bought by the father of the present owner, Mr Bayliss, who advises that these outbuildings were the subject of a major conversion in 1955 to make them into a row of small shops, with structural work to enable a first floor to be added at a later date to those that were only single storey. However, the old frontage to Victoria Street was kept. There was a sign at the St John Street end proudly announcing a welcome to

Farmer's Fold Shopping Centre. I can only ever remember the name John Street being used when I was a child, and of course its older name, John's Lane, was changed to John Street. Maybe this was why local people never used the prefix "Saint".

A major fire in about 1968 meant there was a need to rebuild, and this time the old building at the front was too much damaged to save. Town maps going back to 1871 show a similar range of buildings, to those still along the Fold in 1954, and photographs at the time of redevelopment show some had a timber-framed origin. So far only a couple of the shops have taken the advantage of having a first floor to use for their businesses.

An interesting variety of shops offering good service survive today, with a shoe repairer, cafe, jeweller, hairdresser, men's boutique and greeting cards shop. Also the name Povey lives on with the traders using this name offering a good range of hot and cold take-away foods.

CHAPTER 13
CASTLE YARD

This narrow pedestrian alley between the café Burger King and shoe shop Footlocker in Dudley Street widens out into a small way for vehicles, giving rear access to the properties all around it, and leading into Market Street, opposite Castle Street. So the name is used twice just for convenience, and we have an ordinary alleyway between shops dating from the twentieth century with no connections with animals.

However, if we stop and consider the bits of information we can piece together, this area does have an interesting history. The 1750 map shows no Queen Street, no Market Street or the streets off it. Princess Street was then a small lane, called Clarke's Lane from the junction with Berry Street, and it turned towards Dudley Street and became a very narrow route, perhaps only a footway, which emerged into Dudley Street between buildings. This was roughly where Queen Street is now. But off Clarke's Lane, on the route of Market Street, is shown a yard or court, with buildings on both sides of it, ending in a long succession of gardens from London Row (Piper's Row) as far as the backs of buildings fronting Dudley Street. The end of this

court seems to give access to an alley from one or more of these buildings – was this Castle Yard, where coaches came in and out, and where the buildings along the alley could have been used for the many horses needing stabling?

By 1788 Queen Street had been built between Clarke's Lane and the end of Piper's Row (London Row as it was). The northern side of Queen Street had been developed, and the southern side was being built up over the next thirty years. Buildings from the period have survived on both sides of the street. Clearly it was necessary for this new street to be extended to join up with Dudley Street. The Town Commissioners in 1814 set about preparing a plan, working out costs and buying in the necessary properties. After negotiations with the various people involved the street was completed within three years.

By this time the land behind Queen Street, roughly next door to where Castle Yard is, had become a pig market, in an attempt to improve the situation of pig pens actually being sited in Dudley Street itself. Certainly the Clerk to the Commissioners was instructed to buy land then

Modern view of Castle Yard (Photograph Joyce Perry.)

known as "Fenn's Yard" for a new pig market in 1815. This followed an Act advertised in 1813 which was intended to clear the Roundabout area of the Market Place of the cattle market and Dudley Street of the pig pens. The Commissioners wanted to move both of them to Snow Hill. The pig market is shown on the 1827 map, as is also Castle Street. Bearing in mind the Castle Inn was actually in Dudley Street, maybe the alternative name of Castle Yard was already in use. The Inn was by the end of the 18th century one of the main establishments in the town used by coaches, with quite a lucrative posting business from Ireland. The Inn boasted fourteen bedrooms and stabling for 40 horses.

The Pig Market gave the name Market Street, and it was soon found to be not large enough for the number of pigs being bought and sold. Pig pens were still appearing in Dudley Street. By 1847 the Duke of Cleveland was talking of establishing a new cattle market on his land next to St George's Churchyard between Bilston Street and Cleveland Road. The Town Commissioners negotiated with the Duke and at the time it was reported that more than 3,400 sheep and 2,500 pigs were being brought for sale in a month.

Once the Pig Market had been moved from Dudley Street the land soon filled up with buildings as can be seen on the 1871 town map. Some of these buildings may have been retained for re-use, but the space behind the tall late Georgian and Regency buildings fronting Queen Street developed as a brewery, with its access off Market Street. Next to this, over the yard of the Castle Inn, there are Courts No. 2 and 3, Market Street, rows of small cottages with narrow pedestrian access at the Dudley Street and Market Street ends – hardly encouraging to the ordinary shopper to take a short cut. At the Market Street end of Court No. 3 stood a public house with the name Brewery Vaults, where beer no doubt travelled just a few yards from where it was made to where it was sold. It faced Castle Street, with the Sunday School of the Congregational Church, sadly demolished in the 1970s, on the left-hand corner, and, a few yards down Castle Street on the right, the Pavilion Music Hall, the shell of which remains as storage for the Express and Star.

This layout was to remain for many years. The street map produced in 1914 by Alfred Hinde, the printers, whose main premises were just across the way in Dudley Street, shows the name Castle Yard. The 1914 Ordnance Survey shows the Brewery, and the Brewery Vaults public house, and the narrow passageway still running between Dudley Street and Market Street. It is only when we reach the 1920s that we see the change to the Castle Yard we now know. This was the era when the Council decided that many streets needed to be widened, perhaps by a few feet, and to achieve that substantial demolition of complete blocks of properties would be necessary.

The Old Wolverhampton Breweries Ltd went into liquidation, and Frank Myatt Ltd bought their property in 1920. Archive photographs show signs on premises in Dudley Street bearing the name "Myatt Ales". The Brewery Vaults was by now known as the Alhambra, with a yard and wine store in the eastern side of the former brewery premises. The western section had been sold off and developed for shops fronting Dudley Street, perhaps also when the old brewery went into liquidation.

The Council bought Myatts' property in 1926, by compulsory purchase. Plans on documents at this time show improvement lines for widening both Market Street and Dudley Street. They also show the Dudley Street end of Castle Yard as it is now, and the Market Street end in outline, described simply as an "accommodation road", i.e. intending to give rear access to business premises all around.

Henry Southan's clothing emporium was at 14 and 15 Dudley Street, the left hand side of Castle Yard, and in 1928 Mr Southan agreed with the Council that he would rebuild the shop, before September 1932, with the frontage set back, and would surrender the front bit of land to the Council for road widening. A tenuous link with the clothing trade, maybe, but a date for the typical 1930s frontage to Dudley Street, the upper floor of which survives.

In Market Street the Council also needed to buy in the cottages, yard, narrow passageway and shops adjoining the Alhambra and old brewery. This was

Plan showing layout of buildings in Dudley Street and Market Street, including cottages and other buildings in Castle Yard. The proposed street improvement lines and new road, being the present layout of Castle Yard, is also superimposed. (Courtesy Wolverhampton City Council.)

in the ownership of the estate of Thomas Skidmore, auctioneer, late of Parkdale, who died in 1909 – the name of the firm lives on in Waterloo Road. His descendants, Arthur Skidmore of Tettenhall, solicitor, and Harold Skidmore of Wightwick, auctioneer, acting as executors, sold the property to the Council in November 1924. Behind two shops fronting Market Street the conveyance describes "5 messuages or dwellinghouses known as Nos. 1, 2, 3, 4, and 5, Court 2, Market Street", all occupied, with a right of way to Dudley Street. The abstract of Skidmore's title refers to this as "formerly the entrance or gateway of the Castle Inn." The document reveals that Skidmore had owned No. 16 Dudley Street, and sold it to long-standing tenants, shoe and boot business Freeman Hardy and Willis, in October 1924. The sign "Freeman's Boots" appears on archive photographs, and they were in business at the same premises until just a few years ago. The shop was probably re-fronted in the 1960s, and this resulted in an unfortunate break in the 1930s style upper floor frontages.

A 1920s view of the crossroads of Queen Street with Market Street. The photographer has attracted the attention of onlookers, but the point duty policeman looks away, with no traffic to direct, and the men working on the street surface have abandoned their pick and shovels. Looking along Market Street we see, beyond Rawlins, hairdresser, the premises of Wolverhampton Brewery Company, and the words "Frank Myatt" on the side and "Myatt's Ales" on the front of the gable building. This is the "Brewery Vaults" and the start of the narrow passageway known as Castle Yard. The grand building on the left was Queen Street Congregational Church built 1864. (Photograph courtesy of Wolverhampton Archives and Local Studies.)

Once the "accommodation road" had been laid out, the Council sold off the land behind the improvement line fronting Market Street. The block next to Castle Yard, with an area of one hundred and forty nine and one third square yards, was sold in October 1930, to Samuel Joseph Stanton of Hednesford, baker. Readers will recall that until recently there were several Stanton's the Bakers around the town. Samuel Stanton covenanted to build a shop on the site before June 1931. North of this building, the site of 505 square yards was sold in June 1934, to builders Harry and John Norman Patten of Wednesfield. They covenanted that the ground floor of buildings they erected would be used as shops, and that no part would be used for residential purposes. So here we have a date for the four shops with their 1930s style round headed windows on the first floor frontage.

What at first we thought was a simple modern alleyway, we find has an interesting history. Who knows whether sheep were kept here hundreds of years ago, just off a main thoroughfare, but certainly horses and pigs feature in the story of its use.

CHAPTER *14*
WOOLPACK ALLEY

In recent years this access-way has gained an unsavoury reputation, as a result of the Council widening it and building some public toilets, with the consequent congregating of intimidating beings around them. These replaced the old lavatories below ground level in Queen Square which were filled in. The modern toilets were closed, the smell remained, as did the space for people to congregate. Instead of remedying the problem the Council have decided to close the ancient alley for good, and to remove an important link with the past, as well as an important link in practical terms.

Hampton Walk is a pretty, modern arcade of shops, with a variety of uses: a hairdressers, building society, an inviting café, eastern and western clothing stores and a very helpful and worthy charity shop. But it is a private pedestrian way, and access to and from the Square is only when the arcade is open.

In 1750 the entrance to the alley on High Green was almost obscured by the great High Hall of the Levesons. The passage-way began next to a tavern or inn which may have been the fore-

Modern view of Woolpack Alley. (Photograph Joyce Perry.)

runner of the building which now contains the Tourist Information Centre. The Edwardian façade which many years ago was the frontage of Reynolds' Restaurant, Tea-Room and Bakery, replaced a Georgian façade, and this in turn hid remnants of a timber-framed building. Sadly when the refurbishment and rebuilding was undertaken to create the Information Centre the remains of the earlier building were destroyed, but some of the timbers were temporarily retained for use as internal decoration within the centre. When the public area was altered, these timbers were removed, but at least the evidence hinted at how far back in time the origins of the alley may go.

Around the back and the western side of the High Hall was another narrow alley-way, called Sutton's Lane. The 1802 Rate Book records that maltster William Hollis was based here, as were victuallers Robert Careless at No. 1 and John Barnsley at No. 4, with perukemaker (wigmaker) Elizabeth Allen at No. 2.

The High Hall was a large, rambling, three storey Tudor house with several gables, quite picturesque to judge from drawings of it. The owner James Leveson, or Luson, as it was pronounced and sometimes spelt, was of a family which had grown wealthy through the wool trade, and was described as a Merchant of the Staple of Calais. Calais, as we have discovered, was taken by the English, and became the route for trade to mainland Europe. James Leveson died in 1547.

The Normansells took over when the Levesons left. The Normansells were Mercers who had owned the mediaeval Merridale, part of which survived long enough to escape demolition by its owner, through the good offices of the contractors hired to knock it down, who realised the interior held evidence of its ancient beginnings, and the quick action of the Council in having it spot-listed. Its new owners, Maythorn Construction, have recently sympathetically restored the building for new residential use.

A ninety-nine year lease of the High Hall, plus other agricultural land, granted in 1654 by Sir

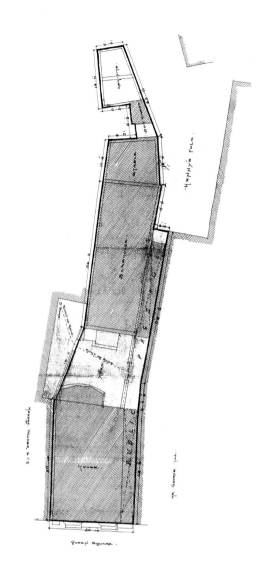

Plan from conveyance dated 24 June 1875 from Martin Wilkes to William Benjamin Reynolds, occupying the premises at Queen Square as baker and confectioner. The public passage, being the narrow part of Woolpack Alley, is shown leading to Henny's Fold. (Courtesy Wolverhampton City Council.)

Richard Leveson of Trentham to William Normansell senior, for a premium of £200 and a rent of £10 per year plus "two fat hens at Christmas and two fat capons at Easter", allowed Leveson to use any rooms he wished in the house. Also Normansell was to provide "an able man sufficiently furnished for the warres" or pay a penalty to his landlord.

In its later life the High Hall became the draper's shop of William Warner, and above it the bank of James Hordern, who in 1780 had come from a farm at Saredon near Shareshill and

Woolpack Alley alias Henny's Fold in the 1970s, looking towards the narrow passage into Queen Square. The three storey 1850s building was the rear part of Alfred Hall and Son, outfitters, to be redeveloped with Hampton Walk Arcade. The scaffold was around the back of Reynold's Restaurant building, which would be redeveloped by the Council for alterations to the Tourist Information Centre and new toilets. (Photograph courtesy of Wolverhampton Archives and Local Studies.)

The corner of John Street with Woolpack Alley. This higher part of Mander's Works marks the spot where Charles Mander first began to experiment in the 1770s. The memorial plaque to the men of Mander's who died in the First World War was saved when the Mander Centre was redeveloped and moved to Wightwick Manor, where it is fixed, a little ignominiously, to the wall outside the public toilets. (Photograph courtesy of Wolverhampton Archives and Local Studies.)

A view up John Street revealing more buildings of Mander's works to the left and right. The entrance to Woolpack Alley is between the plaque and the building which now houses Michael Kirk the butcher and has been reckoned to hide a timber framed structure. Through the arch on the left could be seen the railway track for moving goods internally within the works. (Photograph courtesy of Wolverhampton Archives and Local Studies.)

bought the business of a Peter Talbot. The Town Commissioners acquired the Hall in 1841 and demolished it to widen the Market Place. So the narrow Sutton's Lane was no more, as the properties fronting on to it now fronted High Green.

On successive maps the route of Woolpack Alley seems to have been the same as it was until recently – a narrow passage, which readers may recall was just about wide enough for two people to pass each other, leading from High Green or Queen Square, opening out into a wider alley. This joined up with John's Lane, later John Street, St John's Street and latterly Woolpack Street.

Readers who remember before the Mander Centre was built will know that Manders' Varnish Works extended up both sides of John Street, and up the western side of this wider part of the Alley. John Mander had begun a chemical works in King Street in 1773, and he moved to John Street in 1790, to a property which extended back as far as Cock Street (Victoria Street). His

brother Benjamin, a Town Commissioner, was already in John Street, having started up a japanning and tin-plate works next door to his brother's premises. It was recorded in Manders' history that the block of buildings adjoining Woolpack Passage was purchased in 1778. Here it was that Benjamin's son Charles erected the first varnish shop. From small beginnings Manders' Paints and Varnishes became a large concern with a family history which readers, who have not done so, are recommended to discover from a visit and guided tour of Wightwick Manor, built by Charles' grandson Samuel Theodore Mander. The John Street works was to expand over the next 160 years before all was cleared to make way for the bright new concrete shopping precinct which every progressive town wanted in the 1960s.

On the eastern side of the alley stands an interesting modern gift shop next to the three storey block of old property whose rendered façade may hide a timber-framed building, according to the report which was carried out for

Left. A modern view up Woolpack Alley, showing the glazed canopy over the footway, and the old legend "Shakespeare Wine Lodge" above a former back entrance gate. (Photograph Joyce Perry.) Right. The discovery of a timber-framed wall during the re-development of Woolpack Alley in 1991. (Photograph by, and reproduced courtesy of, Keith Hodgkins.)

A drawing of High Green possibly in the 1820s. The lamp on a forty foot high column, provided by Wolverhampton Gas Light Company in 1821, was mocked as a "mighty candlestick", being too high to be useful. The High Hall dominates the Square, with the entrance to Sutton's Lane and Woolpack Alley inconveniently hidden behind the lamp. The four ladies in large bonnets, sat working at wide shallow baskets or tubs, with tall baskets beside them, are of interest. Could they be involved in a wool or cloth industry process, which was better to do in the open air, such as wool sorting, scouring, or scribbling, ready for spinning? Clearly the traffic and the chasing dogs caused no problem. (Photograph courtesy of Wolverhampton Archives and Local Studies.)

the Birmingham University Field Archaeology Unit and Urban Research Committee. On older maps part of this property was an inn called the Acorn. The modern gift shop in its turn replaced a rear wing of the Halifax Building Society. But older readers may remember this was the back end of the dog-leg shaped J Lyons cafeteria, which occupied all of the original extent of the Halifax. Lyons was the first café where I remember being allowed to sample a ring-doughnut in the 1950s – a favourite for many years afterwards.

It was just a few years ago that the Council widened Woolpack Alley, removing the very narrow passage, by taking out the property known as 19 Queen Square. But Nos. 18 and 19 had originally been sold to the Council back in 1967 for £122,500, and these were let out as shops for many years. When Martin Wilkes, Gentleman, sold No. 18 to William Benjamin Reynolds in 1875, Reynolds' Confectioners and Restaurant was already occupying the property, which was then described as a house fronting the Square, yard, bakehouse, stable and outbuildings. The narrow part of the passage was simply referred to as a public passage, but the wider alley was "a certain fold or yard now or formerly called or known by the name of Henny's Fold leading into John Street at the back of the said piece or parcel of land." Note that a legal document in 1875 was still calling it John Street and not St John Street.

The Lyons cafeteria stood on the site of the George Inn, which moved to the corner of Stafford Street and Wulfruna Street sometime between 1735 and 1740. Before it moved from Queen Square the landlord was a Mr Edward Henney. As an inn, it would have used its rear access for coaching and stabling. Was this the origin of the name of the Fold, or did it go back further in time or even have a different previous name, as happened with Farmer's Fold? After all, it did have an entrance off two mediaeval streets, and could therefore be a candidate for being an early Fold.

Aerial views of Woolpack Alley before and after redevelopment in 1991 (Photographs by, and reproduced courtesy of, Keith Hodgkins.)

CHAPTER *15*
WHEELER'S FOLD

Next to the modern extension of Lloyd's Bank in Queen Square is an arched entrance to an alleyway, a private right of way, leading to the public part of Wheeler's Fold, which it joins at a sharp angle. To the left, the Fold becomes a footway with a covered exit into Lichfield Street, and to the right it plays a role as rear servicing to properties in Lichfield Street and King Street, before emerging into Princess Street.

A wheeler is a wheel-maker or wheelwright, and this may be the origin of the name. Maybe someone who was called Wheeler because an ancestor made wheels was the source, or the word could be a corruption of something else.

At the time of the Restoration of the monarchy, King Charles II was acclaimed with a ceremony on 19th May 1660 in Wolverhampton, one of the dignitaries there being High Sheriff Sir Brian Broughton. There was much dissent at the Restoration throughout the country, and Sir Brian, also a magistrate, set himself up as a secret agent to discover plots against the King which he was eager to report on, whether or not there was sufficient evidence. His reports to the government about

several meetings in Wolverhampton mention Major Edward Waring, "formerly governor of Shrousebery, Backehouse Oliver's governor of Stafford." These meetings at market places were observed to include former soldiers who had fought against the King, and it was believed that intelligence was brought here from other parts of the country. On 24th June 1663 Sir Brian writes that Backehouse, Waring, Daniell and other officers met at Wheeler's House in Wolverhampton every market day for six or seven weeks, with money being brought in and counted, as though these gatherings were central to the cause. However, whatever the organisation's support, no uprising took place. Wheeler's Fold was of course just a stone's throw from the market on High Green.

Facing High Green, and backing on to the Fold, were two coaching inns, the Swan, where Lloyd's Bank's older building is now, and the Angel, nearer to the junction with Lichfield Street, on the site of the modern bank extension.

There was a Swan Inn at least as far back as Tudor times – it was burnt down in 1515 and rebuilt. Both inns appear with 18th century façades in old photographs, and both had rear yards giving access, via the Wheeler's Fold area, to the eastern side of the town, to save carriages having to negotiate the narrow Lichfield Street and its dog-leg. Readers who recall the timber-framed inn the Swan and Peacock, at the lower end of Dudley Street, before the blitzes of the 1960s, will know there was a model of a Swan above the frontage. This was moved from Queen Square when the old Swan closed and fixed to the Peacock, and the name was then changed to Swan and Peacock.

In front of the inns was the old Town Hall, which reduced the size of High Green as a public space. It was used as a theatre until cleared by the Town Commissioners with their 1777 Town Improvement Act. Actor-manager Roger Kemble with his son John and daughter Sarah were well known to local audiences. John and Sarah, under her married name Siddons, went on to become famous on the London stages. To replace the old Town Hall the Swan Hotel, in about 1779, built a theatre in the yard which could seat 600 people. It was about 80 feet (24 metres) by 36 feet (11 metres) in size, and quite plain, inside and out, except the stage at the eastern end, which had Grecian pillars supporting the proscenium, and a painted back-drop supposedly showing a rural scene from a Shakespeare comedy. Those having tickets for the dress circle or boxes would enter from the yard of the Swan, but those for the pit and gallery used an entrance in Wheeler's Fold itself. This regular entertainment venue continued until September 1841, when the owner Mr Bennett refused to renew the lease – apparently it was not profitable enough. It was nearly four years later before a new theatre opened, on the site of the Central Library.

At the same time as the Fold was playing its part in entertaining the people of the town, it was also attempting to save their souls. To go back a little, George Whitfield, one of the great preachers in the early days of the Methodist movement, recorded, in writing from Wolverhampton on 27th October 1753, that his friend John Wesley had preached here the previous evening ("last night he preached here in the dark"). However, in his diary John Wesley was writing that he was on his way from

A Modern view of Wheeler's Fold. (Photograph Joyce Perry.)

Canterbury to London, and that on that evening, suffering from a fever, he spoke at Brompton. Did one of them get the date wrong?

On Saturday 8th March 1760, having been at Dudley the previous day, Wesley wrote: "I was surprised at coming into Wolverhampton, which is what Dudley was (he refers to it as being formerly a den of lions), to find the people so still; many gaping and staring, but none speaking an uncivil word. "Aye," said a well-meaning man, "we shall not find them so civil by-and-by." I wish these croakers would learn to hold their peace. I desire to hear no prophets of evil. What do they do but weaken the hands of preachers and people, and transfuse their own cowardice into others? But this prophet of evil was a false prophet too. For neither while I was preaching, nor after I had done, did any one offer the least rudeness whatsoever; and we rode as quietly out of the town as we could have done out of London or Bristol."

About this time a small preaching house was opened. However, John Wesley, writing on Tuesday 17th March 1761, from Shrewsbury, said:

"We met in the street with one who lent me his horse, which was so easy that I grew better and better till I came to Wolverhampton. None had yet preached abroad in this furious town; but I was resolved with God's help, to make a trial, and ordered a table to be set in the inn yard. Such a number of wild men I have seldom seen; but they gave me no disturbance, either while I preached or when I afterwards walked in the midst of them." This was the yard of the Angel Inn.

In March of 1768 John Wesley was touring our area and preaching at various places. He mentioned Birmingham, West Bromwich and Wednesbury before saying that on 23rd March "I rode on to Wolverhampton. Here, too, all was quiet: only those who could not get into the house made a little noise for a time. And some hundreds attended me to my lodging; but it was with no other intent than to stare." Another two years later his tour included Birmingham, West Bromwich, Wednesbury, Cradley, Stourbridge and Dudley, before he wrote on Wednesday 21st March: "I took my leave of Wednesbury at five; preached about ten at Bilston; about one at Bilbrook; and about five in the evening at Wolverhampton. Many here were wild and stupid enough; however, the greater part were deeply attentive." Such energy and commitment in one day can only be marvelled at! He preached here from the doorway of printers Denman, on High Green, and among the wild and stupid was a Mr Moseley, a locksmith, drunkard, cockfighter, boxer and gambler, who struck John Wesley with a stone, hard enough for the blood to pour down his face. The memory of this incident was to stay with the assailant.

The local congregation continued in their preaching house, which may have been no more than rooms at the Noah's Ark Inn, until 1787. After more visits to Birmingham, Wednesbury and Darlaston, John Wesley wrote on 28th March: "In the evening I opened the new house at Wolverhampton, nearly as large as that at Newcastle-upon-Tyne. It would not near contain the people, though they were wedged together as close as possible. I believe such a congregation was never seen in Wolverhampton before; not only so

Modern view of Ye Olde Church Printing House in Wheeler's Fold. (Photograph Joyce Perry.)

serious, but so well-behaved. I hope this is a token for good." This new chapel, in Wheeler's Fold, was named the "Noah's Ark Chapel", because it was at the rear of the Noah's Ark Inn in Lichfield Street. It measured 38ft (12 metres) by 32ft (10 metres), had pews, with a gallery for the choir opposite the pulpit. It went on to become famous in Methodism in this area, until the move in 1825 to the new chapel in Darlington Street. Mr Moseley later repented of his sins and his violent act against John Wesley, was converted in the new chapel, and ended up a successful local preacher.

A year later, again around the same time, the journal recorded, on Thursday 27 March: "About noon I preached at Dudley, and with much liberty of spirit; but with far more at Wolverhampton in the evening, the new house being sufficiently crowded. What a den of lions was this town for many years! But now, it seems, the last will be first."

The journal recorded the last visit on Tuesday 23rd March 1790: "We had a pleasant ride to Wolverhampton. This evening the rain began, and continued about twenty hours, after more than four-and- twenty weeks of fair weather; such a winter as I never saw before. A melancholy event fell out the day before. The mistress of the house adjoining, boiling some varnish, it boiled over, and took fire, which seized on her, and burnt her so that her life is despaired of. The rain lessened a little our congregation, so that the house contained us tolerably well; and many, even of the genteel hearers, seemed almost persuaded not to halt between two opinions."

The journal mentioned many more visits to Wolverhampton than those above which tell us a little more of his thoughts and incidents that occurred. As we have just celebrated three hundred years since his birth it is interesting to reflect on his influence locally, which has become part of the history of Wheeler's Fold.

We have seen how the Swan Theatre ceased entertaining local people in 1841. The Swan's connection with entertainment was resurrected some 14 years later, however, with another famous person. Charles Dickens stayed there during a snowy part of winter, and wrote: "Snow, wind, ice, and Wolverhampton – all together. No carriage at the station, everything snowed up. So much the better. The Swan will take us under its warm wing, walking or riding. Where is the Swan's nest? In the market-place. So much the better yet, for it is market-day, and there will be something to see from the Swan's nest. The Swan has bountiful coal-country notions of firing, snug homely rooms, cheerful windows looking down upon the clusters of snowy umbrellas in the market-place, and on the chaffering and chattering which is pleasantly hushed by the thick white down lying so deep, and softly falling still. Neat bright-eyed waitresses do the honors of the Swan. The Swan is confident about its soup, is troubled with no distrust concerning cod-fish, speaks the word of promise in relation to an enormous chine of roast beef, one of the dishes at "the Ironmasters' dinner", which will be disengaged at four. The Ironmasters' dinner! It

An early 1800s John Fullwood drawing of Wheeler's Fold, showing the arched entrance from Lichfield Street and St Peter's tower above the rooftops. (Photograph courtesy of Wolverhampton Archives and Local Studies.)

has an imposing sound. We think of the Ironmasters joking, drinking to their Ironmistresses, clinking their glasses with a metallic ring, and comporting themselves at the festive board with the might of men who have mastered Iron."

Charles Dickens liked his Wolverhampton audiences, and used the Exchange building for his dramatised readings. This Victorian building stood where the steps and gardens now connect the lower level of the piazza to the Civic Centre with the Lich Gates and West Door of St Peter's Collegiate Church.

Under the Artizans' and Labourers' Dwellings Improvement Act 1875 the Council purchased a number of properties to clear the area around Lichfield Street and enable it to be widened into a grand and gently curving thoroughfare linking Queen Square with the railway stations. This did mean that some of Wheeler's Fold was altered, to make it a more easily negotiable accessway to the backs of properties in King Street and the new buildings to be erected on the new Lichfield Street. Whilst these do form a grand sweep of varying styles of architecture of the period, and are rightly preserved in a Conservation Area, they did replace a number of picturesque properties in the old Lichfield Street, which was in some places only about fifteen feet wide (4.5 metres).

In Wheeler's Fold itself one of the buildings the Council bought, in 1878, from Frances Childe, widow of William Childe since 1860, was a small public house known as the "Pig and Whistle". This was formerly called the "Admiral Parker", and before that the "Pig and Whistle" again, and it was built sometime before 1848 by John Tombs. The Council paid £550 for the public house. Its situation was described as being bounded on one side by the property of William Wall, and by a dissenting meeting house on the other side. So it was next to the former Noah's Ark Wesleyan Chapel, which, after the Methodists had moved to Darlington Street, was acquired by a group of Calvinistic Independents. In 1870 a town plan shows the "Little Swan" next door to the "Pig and Whistle", so we had two taverns and a chapel all in a row. The chapel was at the back of the Noah's Ark Inn, roughly where the Posada is now, but the reader must imagine Lichfield Street being quite narrow compared with now, so the frontage would be a lot further forward, out in the middle of the present Street. The "Pig and Whistle" fronted on to the Fold roughly to the left of where there is at present an area of open parking.

The name "Noah's Ark" has been used in other places for houses owned or occupied by a church official. The inn was close to, or on the site of, the house of the Sexton of St Peter's. Sexton's Croft in Kemstreet appears in old deeds of the Paget family. In 1615 a solicitor by the name of Gervase Hall, who had previously bought the property from Sir

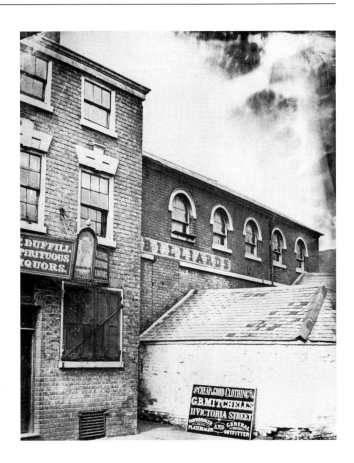

The "Pig and Whistle" public house, which appears to date from the mid 18th century in Wheeler's Fold. Next door can be seen the former Noah's Ark Methodist Meeting House, which seems to have been put to a less salubrious use.
(Photograph courtesy of Wolverhampton Archives and Local Studies.)

John Leveson, sold it to yeoman Thomas Wall, his son William and wife Mary. The description in the document includes the following: "all that curtilage fould parcell of land or backside with all those his three gardens thereunto adioynynge or belonginge". There was a malthouse in use on the site, and in 1750 "a walled garden 159 square yards (133 square metres) adjoining the malthouse, bounded on the south by a certain causeway leading out of Wheeler's Fold into Berry Street and Clarke's Lane". By 1796 the Inn was being rebuilt. Maybe this followed some structural damage. On 6th November that year at 2 o'clock in the morning, a violent gust of wind blew down the whole range of battlements on the south side of the church, together with part of the south transept, and was reported to have done great damage in the neighbourhood.

Just opposite the site of the "Pig and Whistle" was another property the Council purchased, in order to improve access along the Fold at a very narrow point. But they did not buy this until 1903, and it contained just 70 square yards (58 square metres) of land, a yard with a small building owned by William and Ernest Barker, corn merchants, who also owned property to the west of it. This is now part of open car parking at the back of King Street. At that time it would have comprised the remnant of the old Swan Yard Theatre, long since used for commercial purposes. The Barkers also owned property which would be the old square building which has recently been altered for re-use as a bar next to the narrow passage leading into King Street.

On the left-hand side of the passageway, formerly with a Victorian frontage to Wheeler's Fold which is now closed up, is the "Old Still" public house. The building itself dates from the early 1750s when King Street was laid out, and it may have been a private house to begin with, as would have been many of the properties in the street. But in the 19th century it became an inn or tavern, at first called the "Old Saracen's Head". The name "Old Still" was in use by the end of the 19th century when the owner was Jacob Tate, whose daughter Maggie Teyte became a world famous classical soprano. A blue plaque in Exchange Street records her place of birth.

The widening of Lichfield Street cleared away a couple of little courts of buildings - as well as the Street being made wide, the new Victorian building plots were deeper. But the basic route of Wheeler's Fold did not change. As you walk through the archway from Lichfield Street to the Fold you face a mid-Victorian building with the name Ye Olde Church Printing House and the date 1851 engraved in stonework. However, there is a document showing this being built in 1899 as a warehouse and printing workshop for James Gibb of John Street. This is confusing as the building on the site before then is of the same footprint as afterwards! Property was sold to the Council in 1878 which mentioned the firm John Steen and Company, Printers. The deed includes

An 1870s view of the picturesque Stirk's buildings in Lichfield Street, looking past the entrance into Wheeler's Fold, towards Queen Square. (Photograph courtesy of Wolverhampton Archives and Local Studies.)

a previous document dated 1851, when Charlotte Kennedy and Alexander Manlove Kennedy sold, for the sum of £500, to Ann Needham "all that messuage and dwelling house called the 'Old Church' with outbuildings and appurtenances". The existing "Olde Church Printing House" building has seen a variety of uses, but, since 1999, the occupiers, Base 25 Counselling Service, has been expanding. Their well used services for young people between the ages of eleven and twenty-five include confidential advice and information, and they are supported by the Council and Health organisations.

At the other end of Wheeler's Fold, at the corner of Berry Street (now Princess Street), stands licensed premises which were until a number of years ago called The Greyhound. Some readers may affectionately remember Little Austria Restaurant with its individual menu. In 1837 its accommodation was listed as: ginshop, bar, parlour, two kitchens, pantry, brewhouse, stable yard, cellars, clubroom, four lodging rooms on the first floor and four good bedrooms on the second floor. A document of 1776 records an "old and well accustomed inn or public house formerly known by the sign of 'The Dog' including property behind fronting Wheeler's Fold".

Lloyd's Bank was built in 1878 on the site of the Swan. The original design of J.A.Chatwin, in an Italian style, was of three storeys, including the frieze above the ground floor depicting agriculture, mining and metal-working, all facets of the town's history. The top storey was added a few years later. The former rear yard of the Swan became filled with commercial use buildings. Probably some of the Swan's outbuildings remained, put to other uses. It appears the former theatre survived. Certainly a printing works of the same size and shape was there on the 1880s Ordnance Survey.

Probably the survival of the theatre ended in 1914, when the former Angel Inn was replaced by a new building, out of scale with the taller Victorian properties, but attractive in its own way. This was the Queen's Cinema, with its three-arched balcony, elegant foyer and tea-room in the narrow front section, with the actual auditorium behind Lloyd's Bank. Despite its local popularity the Queen's was an early victim of the period of closure of picture-houses, being converted to a ballroom in 1959. Doubtless readers will have fond memories of dances there just as much as films. I was taken to see films, but did not venture into dance halls. In 1977 the dancing came to a stop, as Lloyd's wanted to extend their banking hall, which they did by 1980. I will not comment on the façade of their extension – you will have your own views.

We have already mentioned the "Old Still". The remainder of the northern side of King Street was also built in the early 1750s, apart from the older part at the Dudley Street end which had been allowed to remain. The entrance into Dudley Street was through an arch, which was a casualty of the Town Commissioners' actions. This northern side of

King Street was becoming quite dilapidated in the 1980s, with only a few businesses left, such as the doctors' surgery with its courtyard, the estate agents Michael Tromans and Company and Eileen Pritchard's famous Gallery toy and gift shop. The owners of the block, Hortons' Estate Ltd, in collaboration with the Council, set about a major restoration to give us the unique Georgian terrace we have today. The lands at the back of Wheeler's Fold were incorporated in the scheme to provide much-needed parking space for new businesses.

The 1802 Rate Book does not mention Wheeler's Fold by name, but it does mention Court 1, Lichfield Street, with several names and trades. We can confirm this was Wheeler's Fold by reference to names found in the deed in relation to the "Pig and Whistle" we looked at before, and the Fold was obviously the largest Court off Lichfield Street.

No. 1,   Court 1 – William Ward, Coal Carrier
No. 2,   Court 1 – Robert Davis, Watchmaker
No. 3,   Court 1 – George Careless, Locksmith
No. 10,   Court 1 – William Pool, Victualler
No. 12,   Court 1 – Thomas Green, Wool Comber
No. 13,   Court 1 – Nathaniel Stirk, Victualler
Court 1 – R.Gough, Charity School

The most significant trade in the list is of course the wool comber, Thomas Green. We know that the Fold opens on to an important thoroughfare, Lichfield Street, whose mediaeval name was Kempstrete or Kemstreet – kemp, also spelt kemb and kemm, was a term employed in woolcombing. We still use the word unkempt. In the Rolls of Richard II for 1390 –1391 a deed from Amy, wife of Joseph Jameson, to William Port, Roger Lynedeane and Joseph Wall refers to land with a house in Kemstreet. On the 1750 map are three small enclosures, next to where Thomas Green's property would have been. At the front boundary the map shows a fence line which may be a smaller version of the "tenters" we looked at earlier. Perhaps here we have another connection with the wool trade?

The name Wheeler does not hint at the possible age and importance of the Fold. We have learned that it formed an exit on to Berry Street, which was an important thoroughfare in that it led travellers in and out of the town on the eastern side. The alternative form of the name, Bury, featured in early deeds. This has been the subject of speculation that the Bury was associated with an early kind of fortification around the town as we shall look at in the next chapter.

We mentioned earlier simple explanations for the name of the Fold. When looking at Blossom's Fold, we saw how the name had changed. Is it possible that Wheeler's is not the original form, considering it has probably existed as long as any of the folds, being off a main street, forming a vehicular access from the rear yards of inns which date back to Tudor times at least, and leading out, via a "causeway" into Bury Street. Without early

documents to refer to, all is just conjecture, but these ideas come to mind:

1). The name Bury Street suggests a fortification, perhaps by old earthworks. The early word for a wall was "weall" or "wealle".

2). The growth of the wool trade and the market for wool from the Welsh Marches produced settlers. Welsh names appear in records in the Middle Ages, and not far away there was a "Welsh Harp" tavern at the corner of Dudley Street and John Street until the late 1600s. The early words "Wealas" or "Weallas" for the Welsh, and "weales" for foreigners as well as for the Welsh are interesting, as Dutch merchants also appeared during the time that the cloth trade played a significant part in the town's economy.

High Street, otherwise Queen Square, in the 1860s. The arched entrance into Swan Yard and Wheeler's Fold is next to a fine 18th century frontage, beyond which is the imposing Swan Hotel. Note the swan emblem sitting above the first floor extension. (Photograph courtesy of Wolverhampton Archives and Local Studies.)

CHAPTER *16*
LICHFIELD PASSAGE

We have just looked at the origin of the old name of Lichfield Street. It is difficult to imagine now, but picture the street as it was, say 100 to 150 years ago, leading off Queen Square as a much narrower street than now, perhaps wide enough for two carts to pass. Picture its buildings fronting on to the gently curving thoroughfare, much older than now – some brick, some timber-framed. But before it reaches where Princes Square is now it comes to a dead-end – there are buildings blocking the way forward. Instead, you have to turn left into Lichfield Passage, then named Lower Lichfield Street, still narrow, with buildings on both sides. Those on your left would probably look very little different to how they do now, having recently been handsomely restored by the Council. This route gets you into Wulfruna Street, or Horse Fair as it was.

Stafford Street, as it crossed the end of Horse Fair, became Berry Street, following the line of the present Princess Street, until it reached the present Berry Street. At that time this was called Lower Berry Street, and was one of the main routes into the town, as it joined the road to Willenhall and Walsall. The continuation of the present Princess Street followed a somewhat undefined, curving, Clarke's Lane, ending up a narrow passage leading back into Dudley Street.

So why was the end of Lichfield Street blocked? The theory of our town having once had an earthworks fortification needs examining. The name Bury appears in mediaeval land documents, and the names are interchangeable up to the 1700s. A property known as Honeyman's Tenement, Lichfield Street, the eastern side of Lichfield Passage, i.e. where the Royal London Buildings now stand, in a document of 1724, refers to Bury Street. Even the 1770 Trade Directory has Bury and Burry Street. The "bury" or "burh" may have been no more than earthworks dating from before the Saxon period, with a settlement established and a minster church to serve it, where St Peter's is now. The site is on an ancient north-south route, which would have been convenient and strategic. If these earthworks had been used and refurbished during the later Saxon period, bearing in mind it was a time of unrest and invasion by the Danes, and there was a need for defence, this could

A 1960s photograph of Lichfield Passage when Purser's were the corner newsagents.
(Photograph courtesy of Wolverhampton City Council.)

explain why the name Bury survived. So maybe the old Berry Street and the curve around Clarke's Lane was the outer edge of the defences?

Another factor is shown on the 1750 map – the boundary between two Manors, the Deanery and Stowheath, representing Church land and the former Royal Manor. This could explain the reason for few street connections between the two manors. Horse Fair was the logical one, as it led to the junction with Stafford Street and Berry Street, and the main route out of the town to Wednesfield and Lichfield, known in Saxon times as the "alde strete".

The Town Commissioners, who were noted for removing obstructive buildings and protruding bits and pieces elsewhere around the town, did not tackle this inconvenient dog-leg, nor the narrowness of Lichfield Street. The 1842 Tithe Map shows a building still blocking the way out into Little Berry Street, except for what may have been a pedestrian passageway. But by the

time of the 1871 Town Map the buildings had been acquired and removed by the new Council.

However, the public authority felt this whole area was in need of redevelopment, with its narrow streets of quaint, old but insanitary properties between the centre of the town and its railway stations. The main route for travellers by train was the Georgian Queen Street, but the Artizans' and Labourers' Dwellings Improvement Act of 1875 could give the powers to clear the Lichfield Street district wholesale. It could make way for new, wide streets and new, commercial development, to increase the town's economic activity and prosperity, with a more improved route from the stations to Queen Square. Of course there would be some replacement of artizans' and labourers' dwellings, at least on the periphery of the area, so as to give credit to the Act.

Among the properties bought by the Council in 1881 was the block at the corner of Lichfield Street and Lower Lichfield Street (Lichfield

Passage), owned by Lloyd's Banking Company Ltd. This block had been purchased by the Company from William Fleeming Fryer in 1871, and contained a bank, offices, shop, stabling, yards and houses. The 1886 first Ordnance Survey shows the new, wide, curving Lichfield Street, and the same buildings on an unaltered frontage, one of them being the Staffordshire Joint Stock Bank. Council deeds do not show if these properties had been sold off again by then, but in the next few years they were to be replaced with the Midland Bank building we see today, converted to licensed premises a few years ago.

The small dwellings or other buildings at the back had been demolished by 1886, and replaced with a yard and outhouses to the three-storey Georgian shops which are still there now. These were purchased by the Council in 1878 from Ann, Benjamin, Francis Samuel and Anne Elizabeth, the widow, sons and daughter of the late Benjamin Savage, wine merchant and maltster. The two sons were carrying on their father's business. The plan on the conveyance has four separate properties fronting Lower Lichfield Street, and two fronting Horse Fair. The document describes them as dwellinghouses or tenements, and says that the four were built on land where formerly a malthouse stood. The Council had used the Artizans' and Labourers' Dwellings Improvement Act 1875, as they were in an unhealthy area. Yet, not only were they not pulled down, but their back yards were extended out of the next-door property, and outhouses were built to serve them!

They have been managed by the Council ever since, are Listed Buildings, and have recently been restored for more comprehensive use – shops on the ground floor, and craft studios on the upper floors. They serve as a unique reminder of the smaller type of old properties which were swept away in the 1870s and 1880s in the name of progress.

A modern photograph of the recently restored building at the corner of Wulfruna Street and Lichfield Passage. (Photograph Joyce Perry.)

CHAPTER 17
ST PETER'S CLOSE

On the other side of the block from Lichfield Passage, St Peter's Close is a pleasant walkway between Lichfield Street and Wulfruna Street. The green oasis of St Peter's Gardens surrounding the church on the hill is to one side, the two storey decorated classical Bath stone façade of the Art Gallery to the other side. The rear part of this, turning the corner into Wulfruna Street, is of red brick and in complete contrast, with its more Gothic style, gabled, steeply pitched roof and mock turret on the corner.

In fact the rear part of the Art Gallery, from its entrance off St Peter's Close, was, as we see on the 1886 Ordnance Survey, the Municipal School of Art, and the brick building was the Wolverhampton Union Offices. Within a few years the School of Art had taken this over as an extension, and the School became separate from the Gallery in 1945 when it was given College status. In 1969 it moved to its new building on the Ring Road and was incorporated in the Polytechnic. It was not until the 1980s that the former School section became an extension to the Art Gallery. The Gallery was built in 1884,

paid for by Philip Horsman, designed by Julius Chatwin of Birmingham, with decorations in the Portland stone panels representing sculpture, painting and some of the sciences, including architecture, astronomy and navigation.

Before the Victorian redevelopment of the area, St Peter's Close was a somewhat wider thoroughfare. It began at the Wulfruna Street (Horse Fair) end, followed its present route south, then turned along the south side of the slope up to the church, with buildings between it and Lichfield Street. It continued along the path at the back of Barclay's Bank, and emerged into Lich Gates, which was then the northern end of a High Street which extended down Dudley Street as far as King Street. The Close was called the Old Church Yard. So what has this to do with the Folds and the wool and cloth trades?

The 1750, 1842 and 1871 maps all show a similar layout, with trees around the edge of the graveyard as it was, surrounding St Peter's. The 1750 map has three paths leading towards the church from the corners and middle of the present Close. Each map also has a much narrower passageway joining Lichfield Street from the right-angled turn in the Old Church Yard – narrow enough to be for pedestrians only.

The property at the corner of Horse Fair and the Old Church Yard, where the former School of Art stands now, was sold to the Council in June 1878 by Thomas Burns and Henry Dumbell in consideration of the sum of £880. It consisted of "seven messuages tenements or dwellinghouses with the outbuildings and yard thereto belonging.....the same messuages.....have been converted out of or formerly consisted of a Public House called the Cross Keys and 4 adjoining messuages tenements or dwellinghouses...." All these were crammed into 300 square yards (250 square metres) of land.

This property was sold to the Council under the Artizans' and Labourers' Dwellings Improvement Act 1875, as was the remainder of the frontage to the present Close. Most of this came as one parcel in June 1879, from Joseph Crowther Smith of "Newbridge House", and Mary Ann Smith of Lichfield, an area of 1,362 square yards (1,139 square metres). The price paid was £2,450. There was property fronting Horse Fair and Lichfield Street, and also seven houses fronting Old Church Yard with their back yards and outbuildings. Some of this property had formerly belonged to the Sacrist of St Peter's Church.

The address "Old Church Yard" extended around the graveyard, as can be seen from the 1800 Rate Book –

No. 1 - Sarah Pauton, milliner
No. 2 - Charles Trige, tailor
No. 3 - Ann Stringer, schoolmistress
No. 5 - Thomas Lane, japanner
No. 6 - John Green, currier
No. 7 - Benjamin Barratt, sexton
No. 9 - Mary Clark, schoolmistress
No. 10 - William Evans, coffeemill maker
No. 15 - Edward Francis, labourer

Most of what is now St Peter's Gardens was simply the churchyard, with hundreds of graves,

Modern view of St Peter's Close. (Photograph Joyce Perry.)

some of which had stones at various stages of legibility, some with no stone or memorial at all. Legible inscriptions dated back 200 – 300 years. What is now roughly the sloping area facing Lichfield Street received a Faculty from Lichfield Diocese in 1894, giving authority for it to be converted into an open space. The remaining gardens around the north and south of the church were not laid out as an open space until a Lichfield Faculty was granted in 1937. In both cases the gravestones were taken up, but none of the remains beneath the ground, and in fact there are still small pieces of land which are the sites of privately owned graves.

The Council covenanted to carefully re-inter any remains in graves which might be disturbed in laying out the open space, and that the land should not be used for meetings, sports, games, playing of music, sale or consumption of refreshments, advertising, and that no noise should be allowed to interfere with church worship. The layout of the gardens, steps, walls, railings etc were set out on plans attached to the documents.

The space between the path of Old Church Yard and Lichfield Street was a little wider then – remember that Lichfield Street was a much narrower thoroughfare before the redevelopment. The back part of the Wolverhampton and Staffordshire Bank (Barclay's) was already constructed – it was built in two halves – and in front of it stood a three storey 18th century building and a wonderful three storey gabled and jettied timber-framed building, known as Cholditch's, which formed the corner of Lich Gates or High Street with Lichfield Street. This features in the J.M.W. Turner painting of a busy High Green in 1795. Next to this and along Lichfield Street, backing on to the Old Church Yard, the bank owned several properties. In May 1880 they sold to the Council, for the sum of £3,250, Nos. 2-8 Lichfield Street and Nos. 1 and 2 Old Church Yard, with a passage or entry between No. 8 and the adjacent building. In 1808 an insurance policy with the Norwich Union records that No. 8 was built of brick and timber and part thatched, when George Roberts, a last maker, was the occupier. Stephen Riley, who was followed by a cooper, a fruiterer by the name of Moseley, and Richard Hudson, and his son William, both cork cutters, were later traders here.

Next to the bank properties was a block containing Nos. 9, 10 and 11 Lichfield Street, and property fronting the Old Church Yard, sold to the Council in January 1878, for the sum £1,650, by Alexander Clement Foster-Gough, subject to the payment of Pooler's Dole, 13s 4d (approximately 67p) per annum, payable to forty poor people on Good Friday in every year and charged on the said premises. This relates to the Dole Charity of John Pooler, and the Council had this charge redeemed by the Board of Charity Commissioners in 1879.

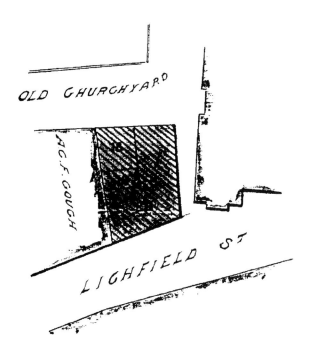

Plan from conveyance dated 18 November 1880 from William Turner to Council of premises between Lichfield Street and the Old Church Yard. (Courtesy Wolverhampton City Council.)

When Thomas Barnett, licensed appraiser, reported on the property for the Council in 1877, he described three houses with shops fronting Lichfield Street, three storeys high, and a large old house fronting Old Church Yard, four storeys high. His report said the buildings were old, but the Lichfield Street front had been rebuilt some years before.

The Gough family had owned the property since 1802, when it was sold to them by Joseph Cotterell, wiremaker of Birmingham, and it was described as "The Posthouse.....part whereof is used as a Blacksmith's shop...."

Delving further back into documents there are found several Dole receipts dating from the 1750s. In 1751 a sum of 13s 4d was "issuing out of the Building the said Thomas Hillman lives in." A receipt in March 1758 says: "Rec'd of Mr Tho: Hillman Thirteen shillings and four pence for Mr Pooler's Dole to be Distributed to the Poor of Wolverhampton upon Good Friday next – by John Snow."

In September 1723 the property was sold to William Riley, locksmith. Parties to the document were John Hillman, clerk; Thomas Allison, innholder, the son and heir of William Allison, deceased; William Woolley, carrier, and William Riley. Of local interest is the following wording: "And whereas the said William Allison was in his lifetime Postmaster of the Post Office kept in and for the said Town of Wolverhampton..."

The building had been redeveloped in 1688, when Thomas Allison, a silkweaver, was granted the site for new building. The land had "a certain Messuage Burgage or Tenement of the said William Allison on the South side....the Churchyard of Wolverhampton....North, and a small Lane or Passage there on the West ..." It may therefore have been a Burgage plot of the Deanery Borough created in 1263, and indeed its 16½ feet breadth may be a pointer to that.

The last bit of property before we reach the narrow passageway that led from Lichfield Street and opened out into what is now St Peter's Close is perhaps the most important, as we shall see.

The earliest surviving document is a mortgage from May 1712. A Wolverhampton widow, Mary Hill, and her son Ailmer, a locksmith, granted the mortgage to William Perry of Pattingham, a cordwainer (shoe maker), to secure the sum of £30, and the description read "all that house Burgage or tenement .. in Lichfield Street now in the possession of John Cartwright and late in the holding of one Thomas Lilley...."

When Ailmer Hill sold the property in September 1718 for £126 to Samuel Steward, Gentleman, the following was added to the description ".. with all such Seat or Kneeling or Kneelings in the Church of Wolverhampton aforesaid belonging used or in any wise appurtaining to the said dwellinghouse and all other rights and priviledges (and advantages) as a Burgage Tenement and all other endowments priviledges and advantages whatsoever....". This would seem to remove all doubts about Burgage plots from the mediaeval Deanery Borough.

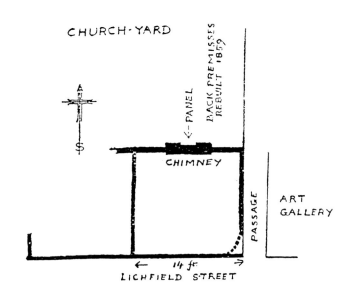

Drawing from Wolverhampton Antiquary showing position of panel in possible wool and cloth traders' hall off Lichfield Street. (Courtesy Wolverhampton Archives and Local Studies.)

The Steward family, variously spelt Stuart, held the property until it was sold to grocer Thomas Jarvis in November 1769 for £155, when the description read "all that messuage or dwellinghouse known by the Sign of the King of Prussia situate and being in ... Litchfield Street ... with two Sittings in the Collegiate Church of Wolverhampton aforesaid thereto belonging and now in the possession or occupation of Edward Gold....".

Richard Green was the occupier in March 1772 when the property was bought by Thomas Pitt for £210. It was sold in September 1802 to victualler Nathan Stirk for £240. William Turner, a Wolverhampton brushmaker, bought the premises in March 1848, the price being £825! But it does seem to have included extra property. The description includes the following " all that messuage or dwellinghouse formerly known by the Sign of the "King of Prussia" situate and being in Lichfield Street......and also all that small tenement at the back of the before mentioned messuage and which was mostly occupied therewith.....fronting to the Old Church Yard ... bounded by Lichfield Street and the Old Church Yard aforesaid by an entry between the same and by premises of Ralph Gough ... together with the right... in the said two Kneelings or Sittings in the Pew Number 2 in the Body and South Aisle of the Collegiate Church....."

William Turner, described in the document as being of Longhope in the County of Gloucester, and a Gentleman, sold to the Council in November 1880 for £1,280, under the Artizans' and Labourers' Dwellings Improvement Act 1875. The property was listed as being workshops, yard, and house and shop, all occupied under lease by James Linfoot, and the right to the kneelings or sittings in the church was specifically mentioned as being included.

We also learn that William Turner was having the back part of the property rebuilt in 1859, when there was found a plaster panel which could have been of central importance to the wool and cloth trade. This recessed panel, below a chimney stack of perhaps a Tudor date, faced northwards towards the churchyard, and carried four coats of arms. The main one was the Royal Arms within a Garter surmounted by a crown, supported by "a lion rampant guardant and crowned or" and "a dragon gules". These arms were borne by Henry VIII, Edward VI, and Elizabeth I, so the date of the making of the panel is limited by this fact. On the left of this were the arms of the Drapers' Company - "azure three clouds proper radiated in the base or, each surmounted with a triple crown or, caps gules". To the right are the arms of the City of London, and below the arms of the Merchants of the Staple – "barry nebulee of six, argent and azure; on a chief gules a lion passant guardant or".

The Royal Arms would indicate it was a public building, and, with the other Arms, we have evidence that the find was a remnant of a meeting place for those who did business in the cloth and wool trade in Wolverhampton, at least as far back as the 16th century. The panel was photographed at the time, by Mr Rejlander, and Mr Turner was happy to say it would be

Photograph taken in 1859 of panel with coats of arms before removal for building works. (Courtesy Wolverhampton Archives and Local Studies.)

carefully preserved. And so it was while he was alive, and indeed when he moved away from Wolverhampton to Gloucestershire. But with his passing all record of its existence seemed to disappear. What a find this would be if it were discovered after all these years. The village of Longhope has so far not discovered any reference to the fate of the plaque. The house where William Turner lived is still there, but nothing has been found to help.

From the Wulfruna Street end of St Peter's Close it is a short distance along the side of the wall enclosing St Peter's Gardens to where we started our tour. From the Barclay's Bank end, a walk along Lich Gates, then down the steps, will bring us to the same place. To avoid the steps, make a short detour via Queen Square, Exchange Street and the piazza in front of the Church and the Civic Centre. On the eastern side of the Civic Centre is a ramp to the same spot, near to the top of Wadham's Fold.

The Waed Hall, or cloth hall, was mentioned in 1508, when the Manor Court of the Prebend of Featherstone was held there. The use of the suffix "de la Waed" appears in documents in the early 13th century. Could this be the origin of Wadham, where we started our tour?

St Peter's Close, or Old Church Yard, may or may not have been a Fold in the proper sense of the word. It certainly had great significance in the trade which made Wolverhampton wealthy. Just a few yards away, within the railings enclosing St Peter's Church, is what is traditionally known as the mediaeval bargaining stone, which may be a piece off the predecessor to the present church, for example a gargoyle or other figure, if you look at its general shape. A hole through the stone was used by traders who could not read or write to strike a bargain by shaking hands. Is it coincidence this stands so close to where those involved in the wool and cloth trade would meet to transact their business?

A mix of old shop buildings on the site of the Art Gallery in Lichfield Street, taken about 1870. The entrance to Old Church Yard is next to the building on the left. (Photograph courtesy of Wolverhampton Archives and Local Studies.)

An 1860s view of High Green showing the gabled "Cholditch's" at the corner of Lichfield Street, the eighteenth century buildings in the continuation of High Street, now Lich Gates, and beyond them, the entrance to Old Church Yard and the south entrance to St Peter's Church. (Photograph courtesy of Wolverhampton Archives and Local Studies.)

CHAPTER *18*
CONCLUSIONS

In our tour we have seen something of the history of the Folds, and of other alleys and passages. We have seen a little of the reasons behind some of the changes in the City Centre, and the ways in which these changes have happened. But what connections have we found with the wool and cloth trade?

Without clear and decipherable documentation going back to mediaeval times, evidence is likely to be circumstantial. But added together, the evidence we do have gives us a widening picture of a town thriving on the wool and cloth trade, and remnants of that lasting until well into the "Industrial Revolution" period.

All the Folds and access-ways which we have examined were immediately off the main mediaeval and earlier routes into and through the town. We have been able to discover where the washing of wool and stretching of skeins or cloths would have been carried out. We have looked at where trades associated with the cloth industry were being carried on, and places where animals would have been kept, even when the rest of a street was quite built-up. We have found out where

trading took place, and other meetings connected with the industry, at least as far back as the 16th century. We have also learned that former names of streets have direct connections with the industry.

Looking at the history of the Folds we have also seen something of the people who lived and worked there and what they did, and connections with local history – the Church, inns, industry, water supply. There have also been connections with nationally known people.

Hopefully you have enjoyed our tour and learned bits of the history of Wolverhampton you did not know before. The study was based on information obtainable from different sources.

Perhaps we ought to be trying to make known to local people and visitors this important factor in the town's development. What about plaques, trails, displays of material, and some improvements to the Folds? Readers may wish to carry out their own further research, or may already know information to add to this book and help build up a more comprehensive story of a part of our history which needed recording.

APPENDIX: MAPS

Isaac Taylor's plan of Wolverhampton, surveyed in 1750.
(Courtesy Wolverhampton Archives and Local Studies.)

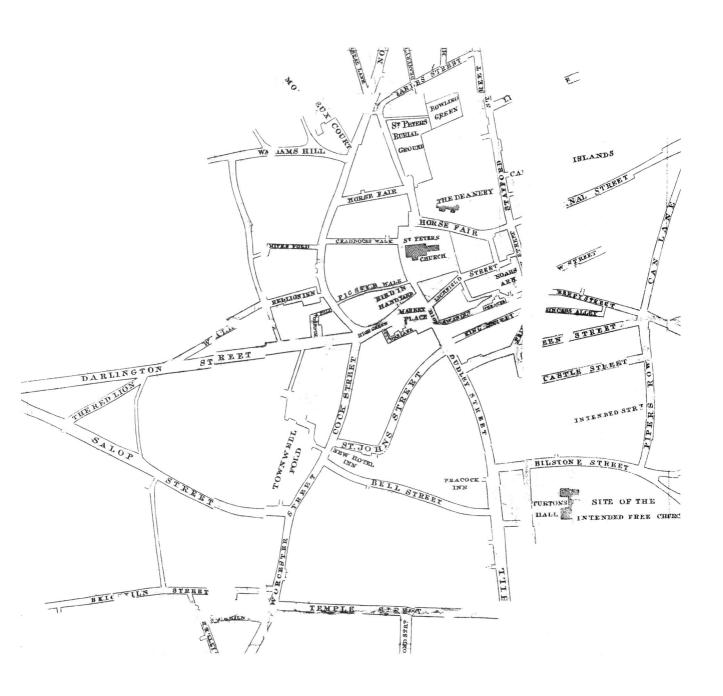

Central part of street map of Wolverhampton from 1827 commercial directory.
(Courtesy Wolverhampton Archives and Local Studies.)

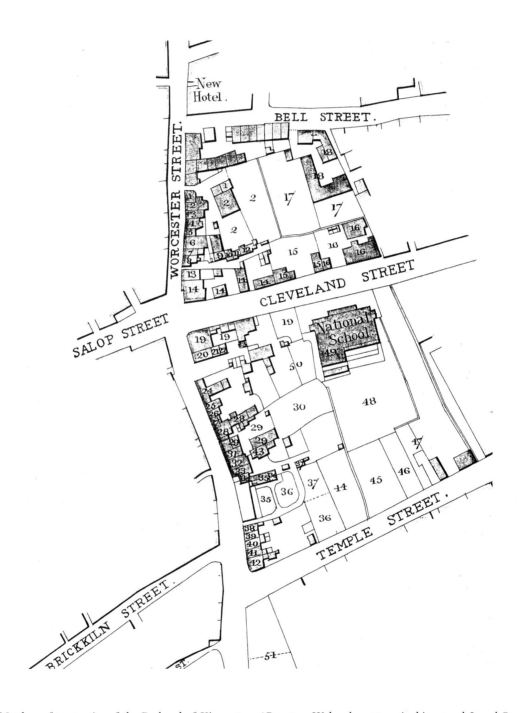

1839 plan of properties of the Prebend of Kinvaston. (Courtesy Wolverhampton Archives and Local Studies.)

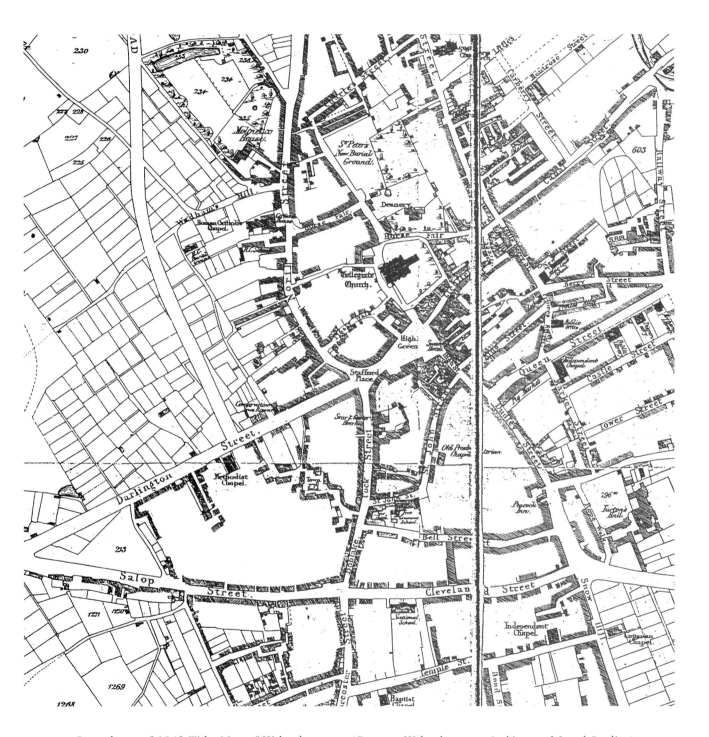

Central part of 1842 Tithe Map of Wolverhampton. (Courtesy Wolverhampton Archives and Local Studies.)

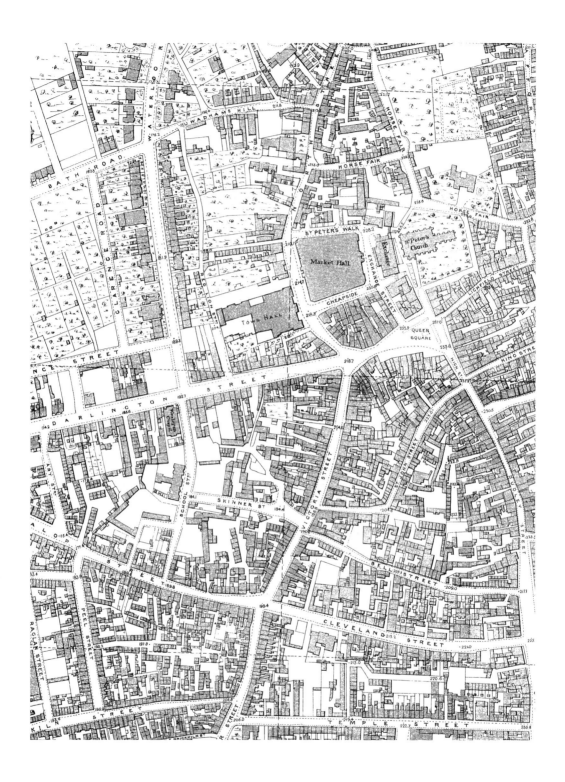

Central part of 1870 Town Plan of Wolverhampton. (Courtesy Wolverhampton Archives and Local Studies.)

1880s Ordnance Survey Map showing Wadham's Hill and Chapel Yard. (Courtesy Wolverhampton City Council.)

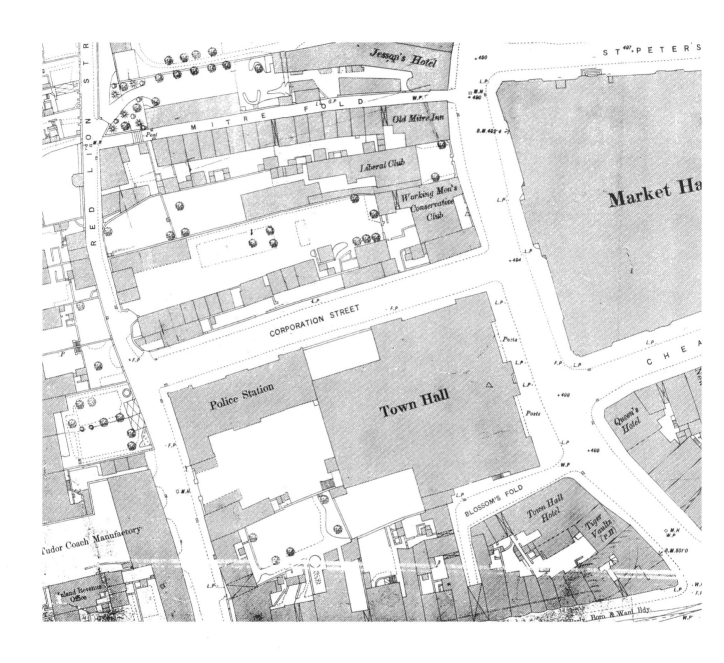

1880s Ordnance Survey Map showing Mitre Fold and Blossom's Fold. (Courtesy Wolverhampton City Council.)

1880s Ordnance Survey Map showing Upper Townwell Fold and Farmer's Fold. (Courtesy Wolverhampton City Council.)

1880s Ordnance Survey Map showing Lower Townwell Fold (Victoria Fold). (Courtesy Wolverhampton City Council.)

1880s Ordnance Survey Map showing Bennett's Fold. (Courtesy Wolverhampton City Council.)

1880s Ordnance Survey Map showing Cleveland Passage. (Courtesy Wolverhampton City Council.)

1880s Ordnance Survey Map showing Castle Yard. (Courtesy Wolverhampton City Council.)

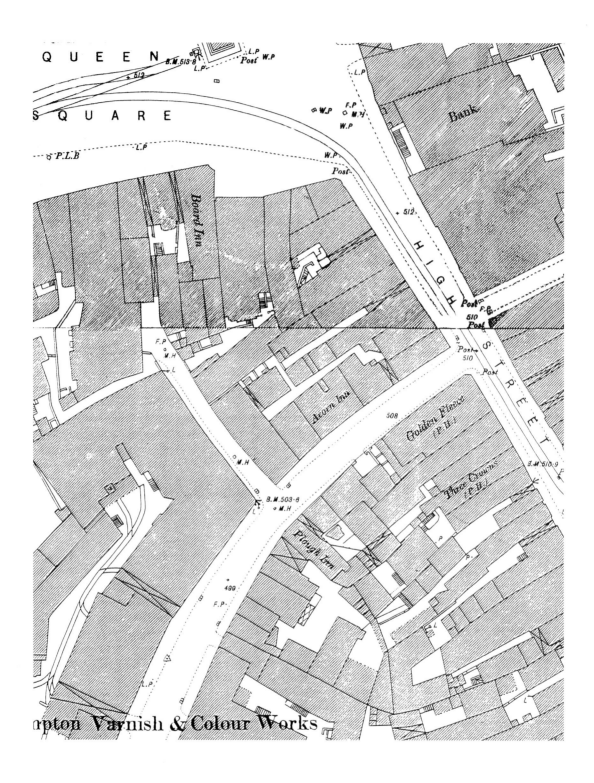

1880s Ordnance Survey Map showing Woolpack Alley. (Courtesy Wolverhampton City Council.)

1880s Ordnance Survey Map showing Wheeler's Fold, Lichfield Passage and St Peter's Close.
(Courtesy Wolverhampton City Council.)

ACKNOWLEDGEMENTS

A special thank you to Wolverhampton Archives and Local Studies, for assistance and advice, use of plans, deeds and documents – Peter Evans, Archivist, Chris Brown, Tim Sharp, Jon Everall and the team.

Wolverhampton City Council – Law and Resources – for access to deeds, Tony Patten, Transportation, for access to old plans, and Conservation Officers Nick Hogben, Sue Whitehouse and Jon Beesley for advice.

- Bantock House Museum - Helen Steatham - especially for use of fingerposts

- Wolverhampton Photographic Society – Jim Dowdall

- Simmons Aerofilms

- James Beattie plc – Richard Harmer and Elizabeth Child

- Wolverhampton and Dudley Breweries plc – Lesley Bunting - for access to deeds

- Trisha and Giorgio Uccellini

- Wolverhampton Age Concern – Shirley Tilston and Gerry Walsh

- Michael Tromans

- Ned Williams

- John Bayliss

- Keith Hodgkins

- Nicky Gee

- Gary Swift

- Michael Webb

- Base 25

With special thanks to Joyce for many hours of assistance in putting this together, and to Professor Carl Chinn for writing a Foreword for us.

REFERENCES AND FURTHER READING

Natural History of Staffordshire	Dr Robert Plot	1686
Diary of John Wesley		
Topographical History of Staffordshire	William Pitt	1817
Household Words	Charles Dickens	1854
History of Mander Brothers		
Economic History of England	E. Lipson MA	1915
History of Wolverhampton to the Early Nineteenth Century	Gerald P Mander	1960
The Hand Inn, Tunwall Street	John Roper	1966
Wolverhampton – the Early Town and its History	John Roper	1966
The Town Commissioners	John Roper	1966
Trades and Professions in the Town 1802	John Roper	1969
Buildings of England – Staffordshire	Nikolaus Pevsner	1974
St Peter and St Paul Church 1692-1975	Maric B Rowlands	1975
The Book of Wolverhampton	Frank Mason	1979
Cinemas of the Black Country	Ned Williams	1982
Anglo-Saxon Wolverhampton	D Hooke and T R Slater	1986

PREVIOUS PUBLICATIONS

The Collegiate Church of St Peter, Wolverhampton, Guide Book   1993
Contribution to text
Published by R J L Smith and Associates

Under the Wing of St Peter's   1995
Published by St Peter's Church, Wolverhampton

Lady Wulfrun's Hampton   1995
Published by St Peter's Church, Wolverhampton

The Fowler Legacy   1997
Published by Brewin Books

St Peter's House   1998
Published by St Peter's Church, Wolverhampton

Ellen's Forgotten Mercia   1999
Published by Brewin Books

Ellen's Bournemouth Years   2000
Published by Brewin Books

Wool Town Church   2000
Published by St Peter's Church, Wolverhampton